# DESTINATION VIKING
# SAGALANDS

## The Icelandic Sagas and Oral Tradition in the Nordic world

Destination Viking
SAGALANDS
EU Project
**www.sagalands.org**

CO-FINANCED BY EUROPEAN UNION,
EUROPEAN REGIONAL DEVELOPMENT FUND,
INTERREG IIIB NORTHERN PERIPHERY PROGRAMME

NORA
North Atlantic Cooperation

Destination Viking SAGALANDS, EU Project
Lead Partner: The Institute of Regional Development in Iceland
Project Manager: Rögnvaldur Guðmundsson
Tourism Research and Consulting
Dunhagi 5
IS-107 Reykjavík, Iceland

Editors: David Cooper, Rögnvaldur Guðmundsson and Tom Muir

Graphic design: Pixel, Iceland
Illustrations: Ingólfur Björgvinsson
Printed in Iceland, Reykjavík 2005
ISBN 9979-70-113-7
ISBN 978-9979-70-113-2

# Contents

# The Sagalands story

*Rögnvaldur Guðmundsson*

I would like to tell you the Sagalands story. The story had its formal beginning during a winter blizzard in February 2003, at Hótel Geysir in South Iceland, just 150 metres from Geysir, the famous hot spring. Gathered there were thirty people; they represented seventeen participant organisations from eight different countries. Few of the people knew each other prior to this gathering, but they had decided to work together to promote historical tourism and storytelling in the Far North. Immediately, at this first meeting, the atmosphere was pleasant, just as though old family members were getting together after a long separation. At the end of the day-long meetings the participants told stories of heroes and dragons, and they sang and danced in Faeroese style. This wonderful activity has become a tradition that has accompanied all of the meetings since that first one.

Destination Viking Sagalands was the first Northern Periphery project led by Icelanders (the Institute of Regional Development in Iceland), and it has been my privilege to serve as project manager for the past three years. Not least among the privileges I have enjoyed has been the opportunity to get to know so many interesting people, each of whom was ready and willing to work toward a common objective. With such a large project, one involving so many people, results can be elusive if the group is not unified in the definition of its goals and the methods used to achieve those goals. As an Icelander, I am very proud of the fact that Icelandic literature - in particular, the Icelandic

*The Sagalands "dancers" in Faroe Islands.*
Photo: Rögnvaldur Guðmundsson

sagas - should form the core of this project. The sagas have long been one of the cornerstones of Icelandic national pride, Iceland's most impressive contribution to world literature. It is only a short time since The Complete Sagas of Icelanders was published in English (see the advertisement on the last page of this book), and indeed, the sagas should be required reading for anyone with an interest in the Vikings and their settlements. Soon the sagas will also be published in the languages of our relatives and friends in Norway, Sweden, and Denmark.

Without support from Interreg IIIB, Northern Periphery Program (NPP), the Sagalands project would never have come to fruition. Also important was the support from North Atlantic Cooperation (NORA). I wish to extend my heartfelt thanks to the staff of NPP and NORA for a very satisfying collaborative relationship. In addition, we

*The Sagalands group in L'Anse aux Meadows, Newfoundland, Canada.*     Photo: Rögnvaldur Guðmundsson

*From Vatnsfjordur in the Westfjords of Iceland, where the Viking Raven Floki stayed for one winter and gave Iceland it's name.*                                        Photo: Rögnvaldur Guðmundsson

have developed meaningful connections in Newfoundland in Canada. This lends enhanced breadth to the project, and Dr. John Hull's innovative and pioneering efforts deserve special thanks. It is, however, Geir Sør-Reime from Norway who conceived the idea for the project, and he enjoyed the sedulous assistance of Björn Jakobsen of Sweden.

Ideas are, of course, the seed from which everything sprouts, and funding provides the fertilizer to make those ideas grow. But if any project is to be successful, nothing can take the place of unity and respect for one's colleagues. The tangible sense of solidarity and the friendships forged among participants have undoubtedly been the greatest strength of the Sagalands project. Following closely thereafter are the participants' will and desire to present to tourists and other visitors the history of the Far North, the stories of our forefathers, and the adventures and destiny that they lived - and to present these treasures proudly, for they are just as relevant to modern man as they were when they were new.

This was just the first chapter of the Sagalands story. There's more to come ...

Rögnvaldur Guðmundsson
*Project Manager*

*The view from the Reykhólar in the Westfjords of Iceland.*

*Photo: Rögnvaldur Guðmundsson*

# Welcome to the Sagalands route!

*Geir Sør-Reime*

In 1996, the Council of Europe established a European Viking Route, fully described in the book 'Follow the Vikings', edited by Dan Carlsson and Ollywen Owen. In 2001, the first regional Viking Route within this framework was established, the North Sea Viking Route, equally detailed described in the book 'Destionation Viking - The North Sea Viking Route', edited by Marita Engberg-Ekman. Now, two further regional routes are under way. In this book, we present the Sagalands Route. Almost simultaneously, the Baltic Sea Viking Route will be published.

We are truly developing the Destination Viking, the borderless tale of the Vikings and their contemporaries into a true destination. That has been the objective of the four Destination Viking projects that have been co-funded by the European Union's Interreg IIC and IIIB programmes. The Destination Viking Sagalands, which is the project behind the current volume, has its first roots in the North Sea Viking Legacy project, where Greenland, Iceland and the Faroe Islands were represented with a joint observer. Today, Destination Viking Sagalands is co-operating with Destination Viking Living History, a project co-funded by the Interreg IIIB Baltic Sea programme.

The various regional Viking routes now established are similar, but are not copies of each other. There are differing emphasises in each route.

## The project area and the partners of Destination Viking Sagalands

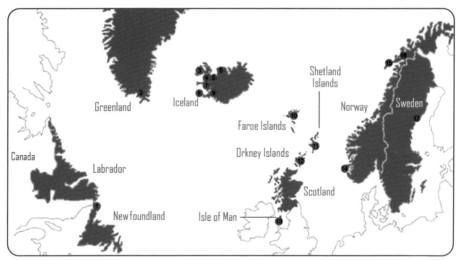

Design of map: Snorre Debess.
NB. The scale of the countries are not correct.

1. Viking Trail Tourism Association (VTTA) in cooperation with Parks Canada (L´Anse aux Meadows and Norstead Village).

2. Narsaq Museum in cooperation with Gardar Foundation and Qaqortoq Museum

3. Westfjords Development Agency (Gisla Saga)

4. Dalabyggd Municipality (Eiriksstadir)

5. Grettistak (Gretti's Saga)

6. The Institute of Regional Development in Iceland (lead-partner)

7. Borgarfjördur Cultural Centre (Snorri and Egil's Saga)

8. Reykjanesbær Municipality (The Vikingship Icelander)

9. Skeiða-and Gnúpverjahreppur (Thjórsardalur Valley)

10. The National Museum of Faroe Islands and The Faroe Islands Tourist Board (Færeyinga Saga)

11. Shetland Amenity Trust

12. Orkney Islands Council (Orkneyinga Saga)

13. Manx National Heritage (Isle of Man, associated partner)

14. Karmøy Municipality (Avaldsnes, associated partner)

15. Lofotr - the Vikingmuseum at Borg

16. Trondenes District Museum

17. Gene fornby (Iron age farm)

The Sagalands Route quite naturally focuses on the Sagas and their tales of Viking time events, but also on more contemporary story telling.

In this book, the partners of the Sagalands project present saga stories and other stories relating to their area, and there is a specific emphasis on places where events narrated in these stories took place. Visitors will now be able to use their imaginary to recreate in their minds events that happened more than 1000 years ago. Several generations have passed, but the landscape with its typography remains much the same.

More information on these sites, the partners and the Sagalands project can be found at the Sagalands website: *www.sagalands.org*

It is also recommended to visit the Destination Viking website, where more information on a number of Viking sites are posted: *www.destinationviking.com*

Naturally, there are a number of other important Saga and Viking attractions in the North Atlantic region. In the future, we hope to add new members to our Sagalands network.

The partners of Destination Viking Sagalands are listed to the left. In addition the  Njáls Saga Centre in South Iceland have been permanent observer in the project since 2004.

Originally, there were some additional partners, like the Institute of Prehistoric Technology in Östersund, Sweden, Destination South Greenland and Troms County Council, Norway, but for various reasons, other partners have replaced these.

Rögnvaldur Guðmundsson from Tourism Research and Consulting in Iceland has been the project manager of the project, with Magnús Helgason from the Institute of Regional Development of Iceland as the financial manager. Björn Jakobsen, from Fotevikens Museum, Sweden and project manager of Destination Viking Living History has been a permanent observer in the project.

This book has been edited by Tom Muir from the Orkney Islands Council, David Cooper from Shetland Amenity Trust and Rögnvaldur Guðmundsson.

The Viking Heritage Magazine, published by Gotland University, has been the official newsletter of the Sagalands project. Take a look at their website for more details: *www.viking.hgo.se*

We hope you will enjoy your travel back in time to the Age of the Sagas, and all partners heartily invites you to visit our museums and the Saga sites all around the region.

On behalf of the Destination Viking Sagalands project

Geir Sør-Reime
*Project Consultant*

*During a wedding at a chieftain's farm at Reykjahólar in western Iceland in 1119 Ingimund the priest told the story of Orm the skald of Barra (island in the Outer Hebrides), including many verses and with a good flokkur (a poem without a refrain), which Ingimundur had composed, at the end of the saga. Nevertheless, many learned men regard this story as true.*
(From Sturlunga saga)

# Storytelling in the Nordic world

*Tom Muir*

When the Vikings sailed from their homes in Scandinavia they took with them their culture, religion and stories. They settled all over the world, from Russia to Canada, while raiders and traders ventured to the Middle East and Africa. Their influence can still be felt to this day in Newfoundland and Greenland, far to the west of their original homelands.

I am an Orcadian, a native of the Orkney Islands that lie off the northern tip of Scotland. Along with the islands of Shetland further north we were once an important part of a Viking empire that ruled much of Scotland and parts of Ireland. Although the two island groups have been a part of Scotland for over 500 years, we do not consider ourselves Scottish. Our dialect and culture are different, but sadly it has been eroded over the years by pressure from outside, and now the globalizing forces of television and computer games has diluted our once strong dialect until it will soon only exist in recordings of long dead people. Yet, when in the 1990s geneticists carried out DNA tests on Orcadians and Shetlanders to determine their origins they discovered the blood of the Vikings still courses through our veins. As a folklorist and storyteller I am interested in tales and where they came from. By being involved in Destination Viking, the Saga Lands, I was able to interact with people from all over the Nordic world: from Sweden, Norway, the Isle of Man, Shetland, Faroes, Iceland, Greenland and Newfoundland. Knowing that Orkney lay at a cultural crossroads between the Nordic and Celtic worlds, I was expecting to find similarities between our stories. I already

*David Cooper, from Shetland, telling stories in L'Anse aux Meadows.*     Photo: Rögnvaldur Guðmundsson

knew that there were examples of these 'migratory tales' recorded in various books, but here was a chance to discover more. I was overwhelmed by the sheer amount of similarities between our stories, language and customs. Suddenly, it was like finding your way home after being lost in the fog for a long time.

Stories fulfilled many different roles in life, from pure entertainment to saving your life. Stories were told by the fires during the long winter nights. There was no television set to watch, no radio or CD player to listen to, no newspapers to read, and precious few books. Talking and telling stories was the most common way to pass the time, along with making music if you could play an instrument or sing. Children especially loved to hear the stories, which were often told to

them by their grandparents. In Iceland a member of the household had to tell a story, read or sing while the women spun wool and knitted garments and the men made items from horn or wood during the long winter nights. Wherever you went in the Nordic world you would have met with the same thing.

Our ancestors believed in a whole different world filled with supernatural creatures and the dangers they could bring. It was knowing what to do when faced with these creatures that could make the difference between life and death. In Orkney the typical night's storytelling would follow a pattern, especially when visitors called. To begin with people would remember old characters long dead, and the ridiculous things that they did. The laughter would die down and the mood

*Alegra Hammond, storyteller from Greenland.*
Photo: Rögnvaldur Guðmundsson

the navy were told, as well as stories of shipwrecks and death in battle. The night's storytelling was brought to a close with tales of witches, ghosts, and the trows (fairy folk) who carried away the unwary. With a head full of tales of the supernatural the visitor would have to venture out into the dark night and walk home, avoiding graveyards and the mounds where the trows were known to live. A few mugs of strong home brewed ale added to the effect, and sightings of trows, ghosts and witches were not uncommon.

You may not believe that such stories could save lives, but they undoubtedly did. Tales of sunken rocks that could tear the bottom from a boat, dangerous currents and whirlpools were told in many seafaring areas. Children were warned where not to play, because there were creatures living there who

would turn more sombre as tales of the press gang who kidnapped young men to serve in

*Listening to an interesting story. Storytelling evening in Reykholt, Iceland.*     Photo: Rögnvaldur Guðmundsson

*Lawrence Tulloch, storyteller from Shetland.*
*Photo: Agne Säterberg*

would carry you away or kill you. The seashore was a place of fear, as it was neither a part of the land nor a part of the sea, because sometimes it was dry and sometimes it was under water. This was where the Finn folk roamed, and would carry you away to their city under the sea. Water horses lived in lochs and streams and would appear in the form of a lovely horse that would let you get on its back only to carry you off to the loch and drown you. Moors had their fair share of trows, as well as mounds, and they were all avoided. Children were kept out of danger by avoiding going to these places on their own. A good friend of mine from Shetland showed me a stream that runs under a bridge and said that his mother had told him that the trows washed their dishes under the bridge. You could hear the tinkling of their china plates tapping together if you listened closely.

It was enough to keep him away from a potential danger, and to make sure he was home before it got dark. As a small child my mother came out one night to where I was playing and told me it was time to come in, as the evening was getting cold. I refused, and she said, 'Oh well, the crows will carry you away then' and returned indoors. I carried on digging the hole that had occupied my attention until I heard it, the 'kraa, kraa' of a crow in the distance. I was inside and by the fire in seconds.

The stories we tell from our own countries or islands share a common root. In Orkney we have a creation myth that tells how the Baltic Sea was made by the tongue of a giant sea monster hitting the earth as it died. Its teeth were knocked out as it writhed in agony, creating Orkney, Shetland and the

*Tom Muir, storyteller from Orkney. Next to him, Jerker Falström storyteller from Sweden.*
*Photo: Agne Säterberg*

*Storytelling seminar in Borgarfjördur, Iceland, lead by David Campbell, storyteller from Scotland.*
Photo: Rögnvaldur Guðmundsson

Faroes. It finally curled up and died, and is now Iceland. As the unlikely hero of the tale had sailed a boat down the monster's throat and set fire to the oil in its liver, that explained the volcanoes and hot springs you find in that beautiful land of fire and ice. Briefly, here are a few examples of stories I know from Orkney that appear in other countries. In Sweden there was a brownie that helped sift flour for little reward, until it was given a fine new suite of clothes and left claiming it was now too good to work for the farmer. In northern Norway a sea monster was distracted by having barrels thrown at it from a boat, until it was eventually killed by the touch of a steel knife. In Shetland a fiddler was asked to play for the trows in their mound, as they were great lovers of music. In the Faroes a seal woman had her skin stolen while she was in human form, but she found it and returned to the sea leaving her husband and children on the land. In Iceland a demon sat on a church beam and wrote down the names of the people who were swearing in church. I could go on for a long time, but that gives you a slight idea of how much we have in common.

What we must do is value our folk tales. Tell them to both tourists and locals alike. Use them as part of bus tours and tell them in schools to the children who will be the future generation of storytellers. Keep this tradition alive, and most of all, enjoy the stories. They are the legacy that has been left to us by our Viking ancestors.

Tom Muir
*Storyteller, Orkney Islands*

*The summer of 1230 was quiet and there was a good peace in Iceland, few rode to Althing. Snorri Sturluson did not go to Althing but ordered that the priest Styrmir the Wise should ride with his jurisdiction as lawspeaker. Now the relationship between Snorri and Sturla (Snorri's nephew) improved and Sturla spent a long time in Reykjaholt and intended to copy the books Snorri had composed.*

(From Sturlunga saga)

# The Viking Age, poems and the Icelandic sagas

*Gísli Sigurðsson*

## The Viking Age

Great events first become noteworthy when someone tells their story. In the Middle Ages the Icelanders drew on their oral lore to create literary works which contained memories from the Viking Age (800-1050). These *sagas* as we call them describe a time when the peoples of Scandinavia used their superb ships to win power and influence across the Baltic Sea and into Russia, even as far as the Caspian Sea and Constantinople. They also crossed the North Sea to the British Isles and Ireland where they established colonies in Dublin, York, Orkney and Shetland. Eventually they reached the Faroe Islands and Iceland in the North Atlantic, both of which had been visited sporadically by Irish hermits. When their country had been settled for about one hundred years, the Icelanders continued to Greenland and finally to the North American continent, where they named the territories they found, from north to south: Helluland (Slab-stone land), Markland (Forest land) and Vinland (Land of grapes). This happened a little over two hundred years after the first attack by seafarers from Norway on the monastery of Lindisfarne off the east coast of England in 793, which is generally considered to mark the start of the Viking Age. The Vikings were fearsome warriors who combined their lust for trade and warfare with the quest for new lands which they explored, settled and ruled. Their scope for expansion seemed almost unlimited until they were finally outnumbered by the natives in North America a thousand years ago. After a few years of attempting settlement they took to sea again, thus postponing European influence in North America for another five hundred years.

The Icelanders wrote secular sagas about farmers and chieftains during the first centuries after the settlement of Iceland, the *Sagas of Icelanders* proper, and they also wrote sagas about Vikings and kings, set in the countries where people travelled in the Viking Age. With their sagas the Icelanders preserved the geographical knowledge that had previously been passed on orally; sagas made them familiar with both their own country and distant corners of the world. Culture made its home in the far reaches of the North Atlantic by setting sagas in the landscape. These areas are still united by the ocean and invite visitors to come and explore the historic sites remembered in the texts with the additional insights provided by the archaeological work that has been performed in more recent times - more often than not confirming much of what the sagas have to tell us.

The Vikings raided and traded both to the west and east of Scandinavia. Towns developed in Ribe and in Kaupang which soon became a centre for international trade. Later, Hedeby became the largest Viking Age town with more than a thousand inhabitants. During the reign of King Harald Black-tooth of Denmark, around 980, circular fortifications were also built for defensive and military purposes. At Jelling in Jutland are two mounds, one with an empty vault dating from 958, and ornamental runestones. The smaller runestone was erected by Gorm the Old in memory of his wife Thyri and the larger one by their son Harald Black-tooth in their memory around 960. In Sweden, Birka was an important trading centre in the first half of the Viking Age and contains evidence of trade with Arabs. Uppsala was the residence of the Kings of Upplond and an ancient centre of Swedish heathendom. Large burial mounds there are named after Odin, Thor and Frey.

Outside Scandinavia, the town of Jomsborg is bathed in a special aurora as the source of legends about the Vikings who fought Earls Eirik and Hakon at Hjorungavag in Norway in 994. Jomsborg is thought to have been on the Oder estuary in Poland, where a town which flourished during King Harald Black-tooth's reign in Denmark in the latter half of the 10th century was destroyed in the mid-11th century. Gotland was the centre of Baltic trade and a large number of runestones have been found there with illustrations which have been interpreted in the light of myths recounted in Snorra-Edda and the Eddic poems. Farther east in what is now Russia, Nordic people (the Rus, as the Slavs called them) opened a route for trade to the south, along the Volga and later the Dnieper, all the way to Baghdad. The Vikings' main town in Gardariki (as they called Russia) was Holmgard (Novgorod). Voyages east of Scandinavia are common in the Sagas and Nordic loan-words from Old Russian illustrate the type of contact that took place in this region: the Icelandic *túlkur* (interpreter) and *torg* (town square) both originate there.

*GKS 1005 fol 79r, Flateyjarbók, from a chapter about the death of St. Olaf, King of Norway, in 1030. Written in Iceland 1387, now in The Árni Magnússon Institute in Iceland.*   Photo Jóhanna Ólafsdóttir

The Viking raid on the monastery at Lindisfarne in 793 ushered in a great period of hostilities in Western Europe. Danes burned down Dorestad, a major French port, four times over the period 834-837, and in 845 Ragnar (Shaggy-breeches?) led 120 ships which sailed up the Seine and sacked Rouen and Paris, and ransomed them until King Charles the Bald of France paid him 7,000 pounds of silver. Vikings first wintered on the continent in 842-843, at Noirmoutier on the Loire estuary, which was the centre of the salt and wine trade. Bjorn Iron-sides, Ragnar Shaggy-breeches' son, raided on the Seine in 856-857 and in 859 set off with his companion Hastein on a four-year voyage of war with 62 ships in the Mediterranean, the greatest known Viking expedition in the ninth century. They headed for Rome, but mistakenly sacked Luna in north Italy instead. On their way back they were ambushed by Moors at Gibraltar and only 20 ships returned to Noirmoutier in 862. Danes led by Rolf the Ganger settled in Normandy after making a treaty with the King of France in 911 and in 1066 their descendants, led by William the Conqueror (known in Icelandic sources as William the Bastard), invaded and conquered England.

Early in the Viking Age, Danes began to settle in north and east England, in the Danelaw. In 865 three sons of Ragnar (possibly Shaggy-breeches, who sacked Paris in 845), named Halfdan the Wide-Reaching, Ubbi and Ivar the Boneless, attacked England and captured York in November 866. Asbjart and Ella, who had ruled York, tried to recapture it the following spring, but were both killed. Ivar had gone to York from Ireland and returned there afterwards, and died in Dublin in 873 as "King of the Northerners in Ireland and Britain." According to the Saga of Ragnar Shaggy-breeches, King Ella killed Ragnar in a pit of snakes and his sons arrived from Denmark to avenge him by "carving a blood-eagle" on Ella - cutting his lungs out from the back. In England, a similar tale is told of King Edmund of East Anglia, who was killed by Danish invaders in 870. York was under Danish rule until 919 when Rognvald, a Norwegian from Dublin, gained control of it. King Athelstan of Wessex drove Olaf Sigtryggsson and King Gudfred of Dublin out of York in 927, but Olaf Gudfredsson went there from Dublin in 939 and held the town until 944. Eirik Blood-axe was the last Viking king to rule York, from 948-954; Egil's visit to him there is described in the Icelandic Egil's Saga.

Around 800, Scandinavians settled in Shetland and Orkney, where Picts and Celts were living, some as monks or missionaries. Many powerful Norwegians fled to the Scottish islands - Shetland, Orkney and the Hebrides - to escape King Harald Fair-hair, who himself is said to have raided Shetland near the end of the 9th century and then given it to Earl Rognvald of More, together with Orkney. King Olaf Tryggvason of Norway is said to have Christianized Shetland and Orkney in 995, although archaeologists now consider that the Scandinavians there became Christian much earlier. The Earls of Orkney ruled Shetland until King Sverrir Sigurdsson of Norway

*A painting from 1862 by the Danish artist Otto Bache, inspired by the description in Njal's Saga of Skarphedin sliding across the frozen river Markarfljót. Published on a postcard in the 1920s and now kept in The National Gallery of Iceland.*

incorporated it into his realm in 1195. The Faroe Islands and Shetland maintained close contact in the Middle Ages; Shetland place names are of Nordic origin and a Nordic language, norn, was spoken there until the 18th century. Well preserved Viking Age ruins, known as Jarlshof, are found on the southern side of the main island, but the main port is thought to have been on the west, at Papa Stour.

Orkney became the centre for Viking expeditions to the northern part of the British Isles and an important link between the Gaelic and Nordic cultures. For example, Orkney islanders fought in the Battle of Clontarf in 1014 and joined Harald the Stern's attack on England in 1066. Orkney features widely in various Icelandic sagas but the Saga of the Orkney Islanders is the main written source of Viking Age history there, focusing on the earls who reigned over it. At Birsay are ruins of a hall and church from the reign of Earl Thorfinn (d. 1064), the most powerful Earl of Orkney in his day. The cathedral in Kirkwall was built by Earl Rognvald Kali in 1137 in memory of Saint Magnus, Earl of Orkney (d. 1117). Bones found there are considered to be those of Magnus himself, and the wounds to the skull correspond closely to the saga's description of how he was executed.

### The axe of Gauk from Stong

*The Maeshowe cairn in Orkney, dating from 2700 BC, contains 24 runic inscriptions carved by Scandinavian tomb-raiders in the 12th century. Among them is the following verse, carved with the axe of Gauk from Stong; Hermann Pálsson considers it conceivable that the axe was owned then by Thorhall Asgrimsson, a descendant of Gauk's killer, Ásgrim Ellidagrimsson. Thorhall owned the ship that brought Earl Rognvald Kali of Orkney home after his crusade to Jerusalem in 1153:*

*These runes were carved by the man most rune-wise west of the ocean, with the axe owned by Gauk Trandil's son in south Iceland.*

Caithness in north Scotland was settled by Scandinavians after Viking earls conquered Orkney in the late ninth and the tenth centuries. Vikings established themselves early on in the Hebrides but Harald Fine-hair did not manage to keep the Hebrides, however, so he "sent Ketil Flat-nose, son of Bjorn Buna, to the west to win back the islands. Ketil sailed west, conquered all the Hebrides and became chieftain over them." Vikings repeatedly attacked the monastery on the sacred island of Iona in the Hebrides early in the ninth century, burning and pillaging it. By the tenth century, however,

the Scandinavian community in Dublin was firmly Christian and Olaf Kvaran, king there from 953, died on a pilgrimage to Iona in 981.

Vikings arrived in the Isle of Man in the ninth century and established a community with its own parliament at Tynwald which was under Scandinavian government until the thirteenth century. From a ninth-century heathen burial mound we can tell that a female sacrifice was made at the funeral of a Scandinavian chieftain, but by the tenth century the Manx settlement had become Christian. Many relics and place names testify to Scandinavian rule on the Isle of Man.

The Vikings began their raids on Ireland in 795 and stepped them up as the ninth century progressed, both along the coast and up rivers deep inland. After 840 they settled in Ireland, building towns and fortresses on the east and south coast as bases for launching raids. They gradually adopted Christianity and adapted to Irish society, taking part in domestic power struggles such as the Battle of Clontarf in 1014, in which Scandinavians fought on both sides. Scandinavian influence persisted in Ireland until the twelfth century. In 841, Vikings founded Dublin on the banks of the Liffey. Olaf the White, the husband of Aud the Deep-minded (the daughter of Ketil Flat-nose and later settler in the Breidafjord area in Iceland), was king of the Vikings there around the mid-ninth century, succeeded by Ivar the Boneless until 873. Dublin became the centre of a slave trade which flourished in

869 and the following decades, judging by references in Irish chronicles. At the same time, the raids by invading armies on Ireland stopped, leading to what was known as the "40-year peace" around the time Iceland was being settled. The Vikings were driven out of Dublin in 902 but had returned by 917 and resumed their earlier business. It is thought that slave trading was not only directed towards Iceland and mainland Scandinavia, but also extended south to the Mediterranean.

On September 25, 1066 King Harald the Stern of Norway was killed, along with many of his troops, in the Battle of Stamford Bridge against King Harold Godwinson. Both were contesting the throne of England after the death of Edward the Confessor. Only 19 days later, William the Conqueror and his Norman army defeated Harold's exhausted troops at the Battle of Hastings. Over the following years William fought not only domestic unrest but also aggression by the Danes, who attacked England for the last time in 1085, led by Canute II (St. Canute).

The islands in the North Atlantic, the Faroe Islands and Iceland, were first visited by Irish hermits but the first proper settlers came from a variety of backgrounds. Different cultural elements from Norway and Britain met and merged to create societies with no direct prototype in the old world. The majority of settlers could trace their roots to Norway and many came directly from there, especially the south and western regions, but it was also common among men and women of Scandinavian descent, who

had been brought up in the Viking colonies in Britain, to leave there for the Faroes and ultimately to Iceland once news of the settlement began to spread. With them were Gaelic people, from Ireland, Scotland and the Scottish isles, as either independent settlers, the wives of Scandinavian men or slaves.

Many of the settlers were Christian, even though Scandinavian culture and heathendom prevailed at first after the settlement. People of Scandinavian descent were in charge of administration as well as farming and other work, and provided the crafts and skills, household articles and domestic animals by which society was sustained. Slaves were given Scandinavian names and had to learn the language of their masters, so their culture was never dominant. Although it is impossible to assess the distribution of different religions in the ninth and tenth centuries, archaeological finds tell us that the Scandinavians in Shetland and Orkney had adopted Christianity long before the end of the tenth century when, according to written sources, Olaf Tryggvason is supposed to have converted the Norse people. Those who left Breidafjord in Iceland with Eirik the Red in 985 or 986 and settled in Greenland have not left behind any signs of heathen burial customs in Greenland. The oldest graves in the cemetery of Thjodhild's church are Christian and date from the end of the tenth century. This shows that Christianity was the living religion of these people, even though Olaf Tryggvason is supposed to have sent Leif Eiriksson the Lucky to convert them in 1000. Many of the settlers around Breidafjord originated from Britain and are likely to have brought the Christian faith to Iceland when they arrived. Many settlers from Britain and Ireland are said to have made their homes in the Kjalarnes and Akranes districts of southwest Iceland. Some place names there are of Gaelic origin, while several correspond to names found in a small area on the eastern shore of the Isle of Lewis in the Hebrides. Thus place name evidence supports the written accounts of the settlers' origins.

## The art of scaldic poetry and eddaic poems

During the first phase of the Viking Age the Scandinavians started to develop a form of poetry which was unique in Germanic culture, but reflects some peculiarities of Old Irish poetry. The art of scaldic poetry flourished in Iceland and Icelandic poets soon monopolised all posts for professional court poets on the mainland. At home the poets studied both mythology and poetic diction, and trained their skills in the complex prosody before they went abroad to try their luck at noble courts. The art of poetry is therefore one of the oldest export items from Iceland. It was later accumulated in a book known as Snorri's Prose Edda, named after Snorri Sturluson of Reykholt in Iceland. In this book Snorri gathers together all the previous oral learning that professional poets had to acquire in order to be able to compose verse in scaldic metre.

More traditional oral poems, containing many pagan myths and heroic lore partly common to Scandinavia and even the old Germanic cultural area of Northwestern Europe, were also kept alive in Iceland much

longer than elsewhere, and were eventually put into writing in the 13th century. These are the so-called *eddaic poems*, which differ from scaldic poems in content: they deal with gods and half-divine heroes (rather than human kings) which are also well-known in the Nibelungen story in Germany; many we know from Wagner's operas. Pictorial evidence also serves to show that this story was widespread over the Germanic cultural area. Metre and poetic diction of the eddaic poems is much simpler and more easy to understand than in scaldic poetry; indeed, it is very much like the metre and diction of the Old English *Beowulf* and the Old High German *Hildebrandslied*, which tells us that this poetic tradition was widespread. Iceland's single most precious manuscript from the Middle Ages contains nothing but a collection of these poems, the Codex Regius of the elder Edda (written around 1270).

These eddaic poems and Snorri's book on the myths are usually referred to as the *eddas*. But the eddas are only one little part of the massive literary outpouring that came out of medieval Iceland.

## The Saga age

As we near the end of the 12th century we see the dawning of an entirely new age in literary history: the Saga age or the Golden Age of Icelandic Letters, which is, in a sense, the forerunner of the modern novel. We see it stretching its influence, for example, through Walter Scott and the development of the historical novel, through to Borges and the flourishing literature of Latin America.

The first steps in that direction were the writing of sagas about Norwegian kings. These gradually expanded and grew, and again we meet the same Snorri Sturluson at the height of the development of the kings' sagas. At this point he is compiling the best collection of all in his *Heimskringla*, sagas of kings from the mythological past, through King Harald the Fine-haired, the founder of the united Norwegian state during the settlement of Iceland in the Viking Age. It would appear that 13th-century Icelanders liked to view history in such a way that

*A portrait of Egil Skallagrimsson, the best known scaldic poet in the Icelandic sagas, from a 17th century Icelandic Manuscript (AM 426 fol), in The Árni Magnússon Institute in Iceland.*
Photo: Jóhanna Ólafsdóttir.

showed how many of their forefathers had not been very happy with Harald's Union, and had therefore taken off for Iceland, creating the popular notion that Icelanders had been a select group of independent, alcoholized, literary individualists from the very beginning. The prototype for these is Egil Skalla-Grímsson whose saga was written in the first half of the 13th century, again possibly by Snorri Sturluson.

The Icelanders became the writers of Royal history for Scandinavia, the earls in Orkney as well as of the people of the Faroe Islands and of Greenland. These sagas were about the settlement and christianizing period in these countries, along the same literary lines as in the *Sagas of Icelanders* proper. In addition legendary sagas about Pan-Scandinavian heroes were written in Iceland and set in the Viking Age: Ragnar *Shaggy breeches* of Denmark, Arrow-Odd, Hrólfur *kraki*, and many others who were probably widely known and celebrated in poetry all over Scandinavia in former times, but are now only remembered in these Icelandic sagas.

One of the major explanations for the Icelanders' uniqueness among the Nordic nations in literary matters during the Middle Ages is to be found in the new and different cultures that came together from Norway, Ireland, Scotland and the Isles during the settlement period in Iceland; these later developed and were influenced by new learning for centuries to come when people transferred their oral lore to vellum-which is no easy matter to do.

The living knowledge of oral stories from Ireland may even have played a role in the settlement of Greenland and the Vinland voyages. People living around Breidafjord, where many of the settlers came from Ireland and Scotland, undoubtedly knew tales from Ireland about fantastic countries to the west, lands of plenty where the Irish envisaged beautiful women, endless wine, rivers full of huge salmon, and eternal bliss. It is not improbable that such stories may have encouraged people to sail and search for land to the west. When Eirik the Red went to settle in Greenland a Christian from the Hebrides is mentioned as accompanying him and after people from Iceland and Greenland had travelled all the way to the North American mainland where the flora and climate resembled the descriptions in these legends, it is not unlikely that fact and fiction merged, leading people to believe that Leif, Karlsefni, Gudrid and their companions had actually reached the countries they were already familiar with from these Irish accounts.

The archaeology of the site in L'Anse aux Meadows on the northern tip of Newfoundland tells us that people from Iceland and Greenland built three viking age

*From the manuscript exhibition in Reykjavík (see page 31), the section dealing with the coming of Christianity which is founded on events testified to in the Scriptures. From the earliest times, Christianity was therefore a literary faith and the Scriptures, people believed, were the words of God. When the Icelanders adopted Christianity in 1000 they gained access to the literary culture of the Church and a heritage with roots stretching back to Classical antiquity. At the same time, new channels were opened up for them to give voice to their own lore and verbal artistry.*                          Photo: Jóhanna Ólafsdóttir

*From L'Anse aux Meadows, overlooking the site in a southwesterly direction with the so-called hall F in front.   This is the biggest of the three halls, with three living-rooms in a row in the centre, a kitchen and two large storage rooms on the right, and a shed for boat repair on the left.*          Photo: Gísli Sigurðsson

halls there around the year 1000 and used them as a staging post for exploring the lands further south. From the butternuts which were brought back to the site by these people we know that they have ventured at least as far south as Prince Edward Island and the Miramichi Bay in New Brunswick in the Southern Gulf of St. Lawrence - and it was in the southern Gulf that the 16th century European explorers experienced an abundance of wild grapes and large salmon in a similar fashion as was also remembered in the Icelandic sagas about the Vinland voyages more than five hundred years earlier.

The Icelanders kept the memory of the Viking world alive in the stories they told and retold and ultimately wrote down. They knew in which direction to travel to reach the different lands and kingdoms. They remembered both historical events and more adventurous tales, and the written sagas present this world to us in a coherent fashion. The sagas can therefore serve us as a living guide from the past when we venture on the viking trail through the North Atlantic, blowing life into the ruins by giving names to the individuals who inhabited them and telling us about certain events, from love-affairs and trivialities to individual killings and large scale warfare that would otherwise be completely forgotten if it had not been remembered and told in the sagas.

Gísli Sigurðsson
*Research Professor*
*Stofnun Árna Magnússonar*
*University of Iceland*

*An Icelandic poet at a royal court. At the beginning of the Viking Age, the complex skaldic poetry emerged, unique within the Germanic culture but resembling in some ways the courtly poetry of Ireland. This genre flourished in Iceland and Icelandic poets virtually monopolized the posts of court poets to the Northern aristocracy. Poetry, in effect, was one of the first export items from Iceland.*

*Illustration: Steinþór Sigurðsson / Photo: Jóhanna Ólafsdóttir*

# Myths and Sagas from the Viking Age in Icelandic Manuscripts

The sagas and poems about Viking voyages and myths that we know today have come down to us in medieval Icelandic manuscripts. Many of these priceless cultural treasures can be seen at the Árni Magnússon Institute's exhibition at the Culture House in Reykjavík. This exhibition sheds light on the cultural and political role played by the medieval Icelandic manuscripts from the time they were written - beginning in the twelfth century - and right down to the present day.

*Sagas and national identity in Iceland. In the first half of the 20th century, street names in Reykjavík drew heavily upon the sagas, and the layout was even intended to reflect their plots. Editions of sagas form the nucleus of every private library in the country and pictures of well known characters were drawn in late paper manuscripts - as the ones of Njáll and Grettir shown here.*

Photo: Jóhanna Ólafsdóttir

*From the scriptorium, or the writing room which shows manuscript making techniques in the Middle Ages, equipment and tools for working vellum, writing and illuminating, and making books, with examples of Icelandic hands and ancient illustrations of the process of book production.*     Photo: Jóhanna Ólafsdóttir

The manuscripts are our oldest records about the mental world of Northern Europeans in heathen times - sagas and poems echoing the lore that was passed down orally from one generation to the next for centuries and provided both instruction and entertainment for people everywhere from royal courts to simple farmhouses.

Writing, introduced by the Church to spread the new faith of Christianity in the eleventh century, enabled this ancient wisdom to be documented as well. Books became valuable weapons in the struggle for wealth and political influence.

Claims to ownership of land in Iceland were confirmed with reference to the accounts of the settlement in the ninth and tenth centuries; the laws of the land, once recited from memory, became established in legal codices; and the poems and sagas that had been preserved in ever-changing oral form became the literary creations of authors:

a cultural heritage that could be cited and applied in all manner of ways.

When knowledge of medieval Icelandic literature began to spread after the Reformation, scholars in Sweden, Norway and Denmark started to mine them for information about the earliest history of their own countries. Numerous manuscripts were sent to mainland Scandinavia, the most prolific collector being Árni Magnússon, an Icelandic professor in Copenhagen in the early eighteenth century. In this way, the Icelandic manuscripts created the foundation for awareness of nationhood in the Scandinavian countries.

Nineteenth-century Romanticism inspired similar ideas in Germany and the English-speaking countries, first in Britain but also in

*From the entrance to the exhibition. Before the days of writing, people told stories of gods and heroes and practised their religion without having books to refer to. Such material was first recorded with pictures summarizing what the storytellers and their audiences would have regarded as the main events of each story. Many of these can now only be explained with the aid of the Edda Poems from the Codex Regius (c. 1270, one of the first two manuscripts to be returned to Iceland from Denmark in 1971) and the prose accounts of the Snorra Edda (1220-30). These two books are by far the most important sources of information about the religious life of people in the North during heathen times. Both are on display at the exhibition.* Photo: Jóhanna Ólafsdóttir

*Flateyjarbók (GKS 1005 fol.) is the largest medieval Icelandic vellum manuscript preserved today, now bound in two volumes comprising 225 pages from 113 calfskins. Written in northwest Iceland in 1387-1394, it is beautifully illuminated and well written. Flateyjarbók was one of the first two manuscripts to be returned from Denmark in 1971.*

*Photo: Jóhanna Ólafsdóttir*

North America. Readers in these countries saw old Icelandic literature as the missing link with their Germanic past. Interest was fuelled by growing awareness that the Icelandic sagas contain the earliest documented accounts of Viking voyages to North America, five centuries before Christopher Columbus. The Icelanders, too, passionately invoked their medieval literature in their campaign for independence from Denmark during the nineteenth century, as a central argument for their cultural uniqueness and national identity. The emblematic role of the manuscripts is the reason that, after Iceland eventually declared independence and became a republic in 1944, the campaign for their return from Danish museums and collections became one of the main political issues of the postwar period. The place that these books occupied in the Icelanders' hearts was clearly shown by the crowds who packed the streets of Reykjavík to welcome the first manuscripts, the Codex Regius of the Edda Poems and Flateyjarbók, when they were returned by Denmark in 1971. Both these manuscripts are on display at the exhibition, along with one of the main manuscripts of Snorra Edda, several versions of Egil's Saga, legal codices and other important works.

## Further information

Árni Magnússon Institute website: *www.am.hi.is*

*"They ran into stormy weather around one headland, and they were driven ashore, smashing the keel of the ship. They stayed there a long time, repairing their ship. Thorvald then said to his companions, "I want us to raise the broken keel up on this point and call it Keel Point."*
(From The Saga of the Greenlanders)

## The captain and his background

On a bright summer's night the day seems endless out on the open sea. The ship streaks forward in a brisk wind and cruises as the breeze slows; the sea and the sky become as one, and the journey seems interminable, as though one were sailing in circles. But the ship is sailed in a specific direction, as though the skipper can see the outlines of the land long before they rise up out of the surface of the ocean. "It's a special feeling," reminisces Gunnar Marel Eggertsson, "even when I was lying in my bunk I could sense it if they weren't headed in the right direction." The builder and captain of the *Icelander* [*Íslendingur* in Icelandic], Gunnar Marel was born in 1954 into a family of shipbuilders in the volcanic Westman Islands south of Iceland. Gunnar Marel's grandfather founded a shipyard in the Westman Islands, and his father later took over the operation of the business. There the young Gunnar Marel learned the trade under the guidance of his grandfather and father and became a fully educated shipwright at 25 years of age.

*Embarking from Reykjavík, site of Ingólfur Arnarson's settlement, 17 June 2000.*
Photo: Debbie Scott

But Gunnar Marel is not only a shipbuilder. He is also a fisherman and has a captain's diploma. He was only 14 years old when he began working on fishing boats in his hometown. The sea has been Gunnar Marel's home and place of work all his life. But in 1990 a minor accident sent him on his first voyage over the Atlantic Ocean in a Viking ship. He broke his arm and was grounded for four months. When he received news of a Norwegian plan to sail the Viking ship *Gaia* from Norway to Washington, DC, he contacted the *Gaia* group and was accepted into the crew as second in command. He then sailed with *Gaia* from May 17 to October 9, 1991. Later Gunnar Marel participated in another *Gaia* voyage from Washington, DC, to Rio de Janeiro, where the UN Environmental Conference was opened upon *Gaia's* arrival. "It was an unbelievable experience to sail into the harbour in Rio; the actor Roger Moore came flying in a white helicopter to meet the ship," says Gunnar Marel. This unusual event marked the beginning of the conference and a new era of recognition of mankind's collective responsibility for the environment.

## The settlers of Iceland

When Iceland's first settlers stepped onto land, a new era of world history began: an era of links between lands that the sea had previously separated from one another. It is unlikely, though, that such thoughts were uppermost in the minds of the sailors on board. People, lambs, foals, calves, swine, poultry, cats, and dogs raced ashore in celebration of their freedom after the long

and uncertain ocean voyage. It must have been a chaotic task to offload the ship and transfer the most important cargo ashore. But the crew must have known very little about what they would need in a new country. The first order of business would have been to light fires, pitch tents, and create some shelter for both people and goods. Next they had to fish and gather food, prepare their catch and process other raw materials, and put food by for the winter. It was also crucial to build houses and other buildings and perform the tasks necessary to guarantee the safety of the people.

How did the colonists go about finding the best settlement sites in the country? Ingólfur Arnarson, the first recorded settler in Iceland, took the posts that adorned his high seat and tossed them overboard, determined to settle in the place where the posts washed ashore. That place turned out to be Reykjavík, the present-day capital of the country. This occurred around the year 870. His slaves were not impressed with Ingólfur's choice: "For nothing we passed through good lands, but we shall settle this little spit."[1] It is likely that the sailor Ingólfur evaluated the land differently than his slaves did, as they probably had limited sailing experience but passively adopted their master's point of view.

The Icelandic settlers came from thickly forested areas of Scandinavia and from the fertile regions of the British Isles. Iceland's geography was quite different. The forests were thin and the soil shallow, and lava and volcanic eruptions only increased the

*Sailing on Hvammsfjordur, where Eiríkur the Red set sail for Greenland.*   *Photo: Rafn Hafnfjörð*

strangeness. But there were other unfamiliar elements to be dealt with. In Iceland there was no kinship network like that which provided the social infrastructure in the settlers' homelands; nor were there neighbours to interact with and to mould the habits that would develop into cultural traditions and customs. In Iceland there was no society into which the settlers could enter, no stores of knowledge on which to build, no other inhabitants from whom they could learn. They had to learn about a new country, create a new kinship network, and develop relationships with neighbours: in short, build a new society. It is an invigorating task to create a new society from the ground up, but it must have been difficult as well. Iceland's first settlers

brought with them their experiences and traditions, and they used these as a basis for the creation of the new societal structure.

One of these traditions was the *thing*, or political assembly. Such assemblies were quickly established all over the country. The year 930 saw a momentous event in the establishment of Althingi, a general assembly serving all of Iceland. This date also marked the beginning of an era that lasted for more than 300 years, an era when Icelandic society and culture were moulded and the laws passed at Althingi were the only monarch to whom the people were bound. Once a year a large number of citizens gathered at Althingi. This annual assembly became the focal point of the society, where men conferred with one another, rendered judgments in legal disputes, and discussed legislation. There was a general consensus concerning Althingi, but matters did not necessarily proceed smoothly. There was infighting among neighbours, and many disagreements became outright disputes, often with tragic consequences. Some were able to further their own interests, others lost - sometimes losing their lives as well as their property - and still others left the country, venturing west to Greenland and following the trail of Eiríkur the Red. Others returned to the east and south, to their prior homelands. Under such conditions, it mattered more what one was than who one was. The son of a servant could grow up and become one of the leaders of the nation, simply owing to his own strength and determination in the new land.

From this soil the saga writers flourished, some of them committing to skin manuscripts stanzas, epic poems, sagas, and tales telling of settlers and their descendants and of the kings and earls in the old country. Some of these stories are as fresh and compelling today as they were when they were written several centuries ago. They have lived with the Icelandic nation for hundreds of years and were written with such artistic virtuosity that the characters became as kith and kin to the average *Icelander*. From the embers of the sagas, the nation would build the fire that would fuel its later bid for full independence. It was a symbolic gesture to celebrate the 1944 founding of the Republic of Iceland at Thingvellir, the ancient assembly grounds and one of the most sacred places in the country.

## Construction of *Icelander* and the year-2000 voyage

Gunnar Marel was by no means unaffected by this unique link to the Viking Age. In 1994 he decided to build a Viking ship of his own and sail it along the route taken by Bjarni Herjólfsson and Leifur Eiríksson the Lucky, in commemoration of Europeans' discovery of the New World in the year 1000. He began in September of that year and completed the job on May 16, 1996, when the ship, later named the Icelander, was launched. Gunnar built the ship more or less single-handedly but enjoyed the assistance of a good shipbuilding friend, Thordur Haraldsson.

Why does one man embark on such a vast project - to build an entire Viking ship virtually alone - against the tide of discouraging reactions from defeatists? Gunnar says that the wellspring of his determination was a childhood memory from his time in his grandfather's boatbuilding workshop. He had always gravitated toward the workshop, and while there one day he heard his grandfather talking to another man about the merits of Viking ships. The man was saying that Viking ships could hardly have been good sailing vessels. "That's utterly wrong," was Gunnar's grandfather's adamant rejoinder. From then on, Gunnar wanted to verify his grandfather's opinion. His experiences of sailing the Gaia and, later, his own ship, the Icelander, is that Viking ships are fast and exceptionally stable ocean-going vessels. His grandfather had been right.

In 1998, Gunnar founded Islendingur Ltd., a company that would undertake a transatlantic voyage celebrating the millennium of Leifur Eiríksson's journey to the New World. The Leifur Eiríksson Millennium Commission was the principal sponsor of the voyage of the *Icelander*. The Commission organized nearly 230 cultural events at some 70 venues in the United States and Canada for the year 2000. Symphony and pop concerts, art exhibitions, film festivals, historical exhibitions, book publications, seminars, theatrical performances, educational websites and movie releases are just some of the highlights that marked the Icelandic millennial celebrations in North America. This diverse

program was designed to promote vibrant Icelandic culture and history and to strengthen the bonds with North Americans of Icelandic descent. On its voyage westward across the Atlantic, *Icelander* called at various ports in Greenland, the United States, and Canada.

The Special Celebrations Corporation of Newfoundland and Labrador, Canada, hosted a major celebration on July 28, when *Icelander* arrived in L'Anse aux Meadows, the only authenticated Viking site in North America. Numerous special events ensued in the wake of *Icelander's* momentous retracing

*Near Brattahlíd, Eiríkur the Red's settlement in Eiríksfjördur, Greenland. In the centre of the photo are Jonathan Motzfeldt, Prime Minister of Greenland Homerule Government, and his wife Kristjana; Ólafur Ragnar Grímsson, President of Iceland; Henrik, Prince of Denmark; and Margrethe Thorhildur, Queen of Denmark.*

*Photo: Einar Falur Ingólfsson*

of Leifur Eiríksson's voyage. On 5 October 2000, when the Viking ship *Icelander* sailed under the Brooklyn Bridge, the goal was reached after an eventful 4200-mile voyage with stops at 25 ports of call.

## Icelander's permanent harbour in Reykjanesbaer

A few years after this famous journey, the ship found a permanent harbour in the municipality of Reykjanesbaer, just minutes from Leifur Eiríksson International Airport. In its new home in Reykjanesbaer, *Icelander* serves as a symbol of the Vikings' explorations, thirst for adventure, and search for dwelling places. It is also a symbol of modern *Icelanders'* connection with their heritage and a tribute to the many ways in which the history of Iceland is tied to the sea and the lands beyond it.

Shortly after it was decided that the *Icelander* would have its permanent home in Reykjanesbaer, the ruins of an old farmstead were discovered there. Analysis has indicated that this farmstead could possibly date from around the year 900. The Reykjanes peninsula was a part of Ingólfur Arnarson's settlement, a portion that he later allocated to friends and relatives. One such beneficiary was Herjólfur Bárdarson, who was granted the land on which the ruins were discovered. Is this Herjólfur's farm? It is virtually impossible to prove that this is the case. But it could be the farmstead owned by Herjólfur, who was the great-grandfather of Bjarni Herjólfsson, the first European to set eyes on the North American mainland. Bjarni Herjólfsson was an experienced sailor and trader who travelled regularly to and

*Gunnar Marel and his crew welcomed in L'Anse aux Meadows.*          Photo: *Einar Falur Ingólfsson*

*Indian chief greets Gunnar Marel with these words: "We didn't welcome you this warmly 1,000 years ago, but you were no bloody better!"*
*Photo: Einar Falur Ingólfsson*

from Iceland. At that time, travelling in the North Atlantic was easy, as ships were good and sailors experienced. Iceland, the British Isles, Norway, the Faeroe Islands, and other countries enjoyed relatively close contact, and Greenland was added to the group later on. On his first trip from Iceland to Greenland, Bjarni Herjólfsson lost his way and discovered North America instead of travelling to Greenland. He saw clearly that it was massive and bountiful land, but he did not wish to disembark, as he was accustomed to holding to his predetermined course. Despite the requests of his crew, he turned away and sailed to Greenland. Thus Bjarni

and his crew were the first Europeans to see North America, but they were not the first to set foot on North American soil. The story of this voyage, however, kindled the desire for adventure in the hearts of the Greenlanders, and it was shortly thereafter that Leifur the Lucky led an expedition west in search of new adventures.[2]

## Facts about the Viking ship *Icelander*

The Viking ship *Icelander* is an exact replica of an old Viking ship called the Gokstad ship, which was excavated from an ancient burial mound in Norway in 1882. The

Gokstad ship was very well preserved, and scientists were able to date it to A.D. 870, the time of the settlement of Iceland.

In the Viking era, a ship like the *Icelander* normally had around 70 crew members, thus accommodating a double shift of rowers for the 32 oars. In the middle of the ship there was a sandpit to support an open fire, and livestock such as lambs would provide fresh meat for the crew.

## Statistical information about *Icelander*

Year of construction: 1996
Length: 22.5 metres (75.0 feet)
Beam: 5.3 metres (17.3 feet)
Draft: 1.7 metres (5.6 feet)
Speeds: average speed 7 mph; top speed 18 mph
Crew: 9 crew members

Construction: oak and pine, 18 metric tons of wood; 5,000 nails

The wood - pine and oak - was carefully selected in Norway and Sweden, and the sail was made in Denmark. In his endeavours, Gunnar Marel benefited from the expertise of Jon Godal in Norway, a worldwide authority on Viking ships.

### Rowing chest
The chest used by two crew members for storing personal items served as a seat that the crew member sat on while rowing. The chests found on the Gokstad ship were worn out from the countless hours of sitting!

### Bow
The design of the Gokstad ship's bow is quite technologically advanced. The bow's

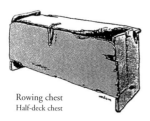

Rowing chest
Half-deck chest

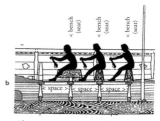

Alternative positioning of rowing chest

Example of space allocation aboard the Gokstad ship

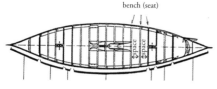

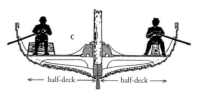

*Source*
Werner Dammann, 1996: *Das Gokstadschiff.*

*Icelander rounds the tip of southern Manhattan at the journey's end, 5 October 2000.*
Photo: Einar Falur Ingólfsson

height was used for two purposes, both for the figurehead - a Dragon's head - which had to be visible from afar, and as a shield from high waves during sailing. On the Gokstad ship's highest deck are triangles that were painted yellow and blue. The carving on the edge of the decks was merely for visual effect.

### Battle shields
Found on the Gokstad ship were 64 battle shields 32 on each side. These were tied to the ship and used by crew members for defence during sea and land battles.

[1] *The Book of Settlements [Landnámabók, SH9], vol. 1,* Hid íslenzka fornritafélag, Reykjavík 1968.
[2] *Saga of the Greenlanders [Grænlendingasaga],* Chapters 1-3.

### Further information
*www.reykjanesbaer.is*

*"Here I [Egil] set up this scorn-pole and turn its scorn upon King Eirik [Bloodaxe] and Queen Gunnhild"* - then turned the horse's head to face land - *"and I turn its scorn upon the nature spirits that inhabit this land, sending them all astray so that none of them shall find its resting-place by chance or design until they have driven King Eirik and Gunnhild from this land."*
(From Egil's Saga)

## Snorri Sturluson

Egil's saga has often been attributed to the medieval writer Snorri Sturluson. Snorri ruled in Borgarfjordur during the age of the Sturlungar family (13th century) and lived both at Borg and in Reykholt. In Reykholt stands now the recently built Snorrastofa, a cultural centre and an institution for research in medieval studies and ancient stories. This centre is partly based upon the work and ideas of Snorri. He was the author of several grand works of the ancient Icelandic literature, such as Heimskringla (the history of the Norwegian kings), and Edda or Snorra-Edda, a priceless source of information on how the ancestors of the Icelandic people viewed and explained the world in which they lived. Not only was

*Snorri's geothermal pool in Reykholt.*

Photo: Björn Húnbogi Sveinsson

*Tourists in Reykholt view the statue of Snorri by the Norwegian sculptor Gustav Vigeland.*
Photo: Bergur Þorgeirsson

Snorri a brilliant author, he was also a chief over the Borgarfjordur region, sitting in Reykholt which was an important place; the chief's house in the region. Snorri had tremendous power and wealth, and had many men under his command. At that time in Reykholt, Snorri wrote some of the jewels of medieval literature, settled disputes amongst farmers and other local folk and played the role of a politician, often against other chiefs in Iceland, some of whom were from his own family. The history of Snorri and Reykholt, along with the whole history of Iceland, are twined together. He lived in turbulent and ferocious times and in later life was in conflicts with King Hakon of Norway. Snorri continued to rule from Reykholt against the king's will. In the year of 1241 Snorri's former son-in-law, Gissur, went against him with a troop of men and killed him in his home after he had made an attempt to hide from Gissur and his men. Snorri's last words are one of the most famous in Icelandic history; as he looked upon the blade that was to kill him he said: "Do not strike!"

When looking upon the history of the place and the importance of Snorri Sturluson as a scholar and an author, there is no wonder that Snorrastofa was founded at Reykholt. The building of Snorrastofa went hand in hand with the building of the new church at Reykholt, both magnificent

*A golden ring, found in the old church ruins in Reykholt during the archaeological excavation in the summer of 2005.*
Photo: Þorkell Þorkelsson

buildings. The founding of these two buildings took place in 1988, the building of the church was completed in 1996, and the premises of Snorrastofa in the year 2000.

Snorrastofa houses, amongst other things, an information centre for tourists and an exhibition on the history of Reykholt and the life and works of Snorri, including some artefacts that have been discovered during an excavation at the site of Reykholt.

Among the oldest preserved structures in Iceland is Snorralaug, a medieval geothermal pool and a tunnel which led from the pool to Snorri's house. The earliest description of this pool in its modern form is dated to the early 18th century. It has been repaired countless

*Archaeological excavation in Reykholt, summer 2005. Church site.*      Photo: Bergur Þorgeirsson

*The view from Borg, the home of Egil Skalla-Grímsson.*                    Photo: Ásthildur Magnúsdóttir

times through the centuries and is now on the list of protected monuments in Iceland.

Reykholt is historically a very important place, especially as a church site through the ages. It has always been a rich site for artefacts relating to Christianity, and many of the most valuable pieces belonging to the Icelandic national church come from Reykholt. One of those is the Reykholtsmáldagi, the oldest known parchment belonging to the church, dating from the 12th century. Reykholtsmáldagi is now preserved in the National Archives.

## Egil Skalla-Grímsson

As mentioned before, Snorri Sturluson was not the only hero to ride the paths of Borgarfjördur. Even earlier Egil the son of the settler Skalla-Grímur Kveldúlfsson, recited his immortal poetry, raged and plundered in the east and worked for the king of England himself.

Egil Skalla-Grímsson would without a doubt grab people's attention if he was seen anywhere today, as he did amongst the people of his time. He was described as the ugliest of all men and Egil never kept a low profile, wherever he found himself. Egil was a brilliant poet, so brilliant that he gained his first reward for a well spoken poem at the age of three. His family had ridden off for a party, held by Skalla-Grímur's father-in-law. Egil immensely disliked being left behind, even though he was only three years old. He saddled up a horse and followed his people to the party, close enough to follow, far away enough not to be seen. He reached the party, and his grandfather was so impressed by the young Egil that he was allowed to stay. Egil then recited a poem to his grandfather, and was rewarded with three sea shells and an egg from a duck. Few people are thought to have received such an honour at such an early age.

Egil was only seven years old when he first killed a man, at an ice-game similar to modern ice-hockey on the river Hvítá in Borgarfjordur. Grímur Heggson, a local boy, aged ten, drove Egil down on the ice and threatened to give him a beating if he would not behave in the game. Their interaction came to a brutal end when Egil drove his axe into the head of young Grímur.

Egil's mother, Bera, saw the makings of a Viking in the boy and she would be proven right. Egil and his brother Thorolfur, raided heavily in the east, as well as many other places and found great wealth there.

The prospect of wealth led to Egil and Thorolfur becoming loyal to King Aðalsteinn (Athelstan) of England who badly needed more warriors. The king was impressed by the brothers and eventually hired them to guard his lands. In a battle against Olafur, the king of Scotland who raided England at

*Cairn by Brak's Sound in Borgarnes.*
Photo: Sigríður Margrét Guðmundsdóttir

the time, Thorolfur was killed. Egil buried his brother in England, but longed for home after his brother's death. He and King Athelstan parted as dear friends, and Egil brought home two chests full of silver intended for Skalla-Grímur as reparation for his son's death. After returning to Iceland, Egil married Asgerdur, the widow of his brother. They lived at Borg and prospered well together. They had many children, better told of in Egil's Saga.

The saga of Egil is a complex and vibrant intertwining tale of battles and love, magic and witchcraft, one of the most graphic of the settlement sagas.

*The Settlement Centre in Borgarnes.*                    *Drawing: Sigurður Valur Sigurðsson*

## The Settlement Centre in Borgarnes

In the length and breadth of Iceland's remarkable history, perhaps the single most outstanding period is the time of settlement. This extraordinary time was when Nordic adventurers not only discovered this remote island in the far north of the Atlantic but also had the courage to commence regular sailings there, and to explore and settle it. These extraordinary events occurred from about 850AD to 930AD during periods referred to as the Age of the Settlement. The history of the settlement of Iceland is the story of how 40 to 50 thousand individuals sailed in open boats from Norway, Britain and Ireland and founded a new society on an uninhabited island in the far north of the Atlantic Ocean during a period of just 50 to 60 years. The Saga of the Settlement of Iceland. Iceland's access to such a well-documented history of its own foundation is unique. Through the Íslendingabók (Book of Icelanders) by Ari the Wise and in particular Landnáma (the Book of Settlement) we have detailed accounts of the principal settlers for every part of the country.

The most colourful of all the saga heroes was Egil Skalla-Grimsson. His father, Skalla-Grímur, was one of the very first of the

and introduces visitors to the saga of Egil Skalla-Grímsson. The Centre is home to two major exhibitions: The Settlement of Iceland and The Saga of Egil Skalla-Grímsson. On the upper floor there is a performance space, The Saga Loft, where storytellers perform and theatrical events are staged. The first of the two exhibitions, The Settlement of Iceland, depicts how Iceland was discovered, how the Vikings navigated the open ocean and why they abandoned their homelands in Norway. It tells of the first men to set foot on the island and how the land was settled up to the establishment of the first parliament in the world, the Althing, at Thingvellir in 930AD. The second exhibition, The Saga of Egil Skalla-Grimsson, profiles the hero Egil.

## How to get there

The township of Borgarnes, where The Icelandic Settlement Centre is situated, lies on the west coast of Iceland approximately eighty kilometres north of the capital, Reykjavik. Beeing the This setting for Egils Saga this historical context combined with the charming natural beauty of the site make it an ideal location for the Centre. The journey from Reykjavik to Borgarnes passes through the lush west coast farming land and from Borgarnes extend the arterial routes to the north and west of the country.

## Further information

*www.reykholt.is*
*www.snorrastofa.is*
*www.landnam.is*

Viking settlers and the one who claimed land in Borgarfjordur. Egil himself was a larger than life character who was both a great poet and also a fierce warrior and Viking. Egils Saga thus provides a perfect vehicle for following one family clan as they settled in Iceland.

To tell the history of this remarkable period The Icelandic Settlement Centre has been founded in the township of Borgarnes on the west coast of Iceland.

The Settlement Centre is a building devoted to recreating Iceland's earliest days

*Most likely born at Eiríksstadir in Dalasýsla, Leif the Lucky (Leifur Eiríksson) became the first European to discover America when he sailed west from Greenland in the year 1000, to explore land which Bjarni Herjolfsson had sighted there.  14-15 years earlier his family, lead by his father Eirík the Red, had left West Iceland to settle in Greenland.*

## The settlement of Iceland

Iceland was settled from 874-930, largely by proud farmers seeking freedom from the tyranny of King Harald Fair-hair of Norway, although many pioneers, especially those who made their homes in West Iceland, came from the Viking settlements in Ireland and the British Isles. Some were simply adventurers using navigational advances to seek out new lands. Around four hundred of the original settlers are known by name and Iceland's population has been estimated at 10-20,000 by the year 930, when the Althing - the world's oldest national parliament - was founded. Many settlers chose where to live by throwing their high-seat pillars overboard as they approached land, for the gods to wash ashore at a suitable place.

*Welcome to Eiríksstadir!*

*Photo: Helga H. Ágústsdóttir*

## The settlement of Dalasýsla

It was generally men who claimed land, but some female settlers are known from the Sagas and other sources. Undoubtedly the greatest of them was Aud the Deep-minded, who arrived from Norway after many years in Ireland, Scotland and the Faroe Islands. She claimed what is now Dalasýsla and later shared out the land there among her family and friends and even her freed slaves. Many places in Dalasýsla still bear the names given to them by the first settlers: Geirmund Hell-skin lived at Skarð, Steinólf the Short in Fagridalur, and Olaf Belly and Gils Ship-nose at Saurbær.

Few parts of Iceland are as rich in history as Dalasýsla, where records go back virtually unbroken to the settlement in the 9th and 10th centuries.

The district played a key role in early links with the Viking settlements in Britain and Ireland as well as serving as the base for the settlement of Greenland which led to the discovery of the New World. Women played a particularly prominent part in the fateful events of early life in Dalasýsla, as recounted in the classic Saga of the People of Laxárdal.

Saga writing has strong roots in Dalasýsla too, since Iceland's most famous medieval author and historian, Snorri Sturluson, was born at the ancient farmstead at Hvammur, which in fact was home to one of the central families in the thirteenth-century civil war.

*By the excacvated ruins of Eiríksstadir framhouse. The replica house and Haukadalur Lake in the background.*                 Photo: Rögnvaldur Guðmundsson

## Laxdæla - the Saga of the People of Laxárdal

One of the masterpieces of medieval literature, Laxdæla (the Saga of the People of Laxárdal) is largely set in Dalir (Dalasýsla). This romantic tragedy is so "feminist" in outlook that many scholars claim it must have been written by a woman. Its heroine, Gudrún Ósvifsdóttir, was married four times, but the centre of the action is the "love triangle" which ends when her third husband, Bolli, kills her former suitor Kjartan, the grandson of an Irish princess, at Gudrún's own instigation. In old age she summed up her life in words which have become proverbial in Iceland: "The one I loved most, I treated the worst."

## Eirík the Red and Leif the Lucky

The 13th century Book of Settlements describes how Eirík the Red and his father were exiled from Jaeren in Norway for slaying men, and settled at Hornstrandir in northwest Iceland. However, the Book of Icelanders, written a century earlier, suggests that Eirík the Red was born in Iceland. When his father died Eirík moved to the valleys of Breidafjördur and married Thjódhild from Vatn in Haukadalur, whose father was of Irish descent. They built a home at Eiríksstadir and their sons Leif, Thorvald and Thorstein were presumably born there, since they were adults when the first voyage to America was made in the year 1000, 14-15 years after Eirík left West Iceland to settle in Greenland.

Leif Eiríksson was the first European to reach America, which he named Vínland ("Wineland the Good"), in the year 1000. He first made land at Helluland and Markland (Baffin Island and Labrador), but Vínland itself has been identified at various sites ranging from modern-day Québec to New York. Leif, who earned the nickname "the Lucky" after rescuing 15 shipwrecked sailors, ranks with the greatest explorers in history. One saga says that he was a Christian missionary in Greenland and became leader of the Viking settlement there after his father. His mother Thjódhild converted to Christianity and had a church built in Brattahlid in Greenland, where a replica has now been built modelled on the original ruins. Eirík's other sons are also linked with the discovery of America. Thorvald was killed there by an Indian arrow, while Thorstein died in Greenland but his widow,

*Training with a bow and an arrow.*
Photo: Helga H. Ágústsdóttir

*The president of Iceland visit "Eirík the Red".*
*Photo: Magnús Hjörleifsson*

Gudríd Thorbjarnardóttir, remarried and attempted to settle in America, where she gave birth to the first child of European descent in the New World. Statues commemorating Guðríð are found at her birthplace in Laugarbrekka, by Hellnar, on Snæfellsnes peninsula, and at Glaumbær in Skagafjördur, where she and her son Snorri lived after returning from America.

### Eiríksstadir ruins and replica farmhouse

The Eiríksstadir ruins were excavated in 1895 and 1938, and again most recently in the summers of 1997-2001. Excavations by archaeologists from the National Museum of Iceland in 1997 revealed the existence of a farmhouse with an interior area of 50 m² (4 x 12.5 m). Dating from the 10th century, the ruins are on public view. Studies indicate that the Eiríksstadir farmhouse was only lived

in for one or two decades. A long fireplace was in the centre of the floor and 0.9 m seats were set into the walls. A smaller farmhouse would have been built there to begin with, and then added to.

A replica of Eirík and Thjódhild's farmhouse has been built on the eastern part of Stóra-Vatnshorn, some 100 m from the ruins. It is a conjectural reconstruction of a Settlement Age farmstead, with its layout, outlines of walls, entrance and long fireplace based on findings from the excavated ruins. The farmhouse was built on a local initiative with assistance from an advisory committee of archaeologists from the National Museum. The structure of the building was based on the oldest known types from Iceland, as well as studies made both in Iceland and neighbouring countries. Panelling is used for the interior and the ceiling has rafters and a brushwood lining, with a triple layer of turf to form the roof. The walls are turf-built using clumps with twine between them, probably the original building technique as revealed during excavation. All the timber used is driftwood. The house was built using models of Settlement Age tools which were reconstructed based on archaeological finds or ancient descriptions. In texture the timber resembles the original and all the carvings and decoration are based on models from the same time.

### Bringing Vikings to Life

Eiríksstadir features a living presentation of Viking culture, with guides in Viking Age costume describing the people who originally lived there and the life-style during the Age

*Icelandic horse, lamb and modern Vikings.*                    *Photo: Helga H. Ágústsdóttir*

of Settlement. There are good disabled access and toilet facilities, as well as detailed information panels at the car park and beside the ruins and reconstructed building.

The Leif Eiríksson Heritage Festival is held the second weekend in July.

## Right beside the Ring Road

Tucked away inland from Hvammsfjördur at the head of Breidafjördur Bay in West Iceland is Dalasýsla, one of the best-kept secrets of travelling in Iceland.

Dalasýsla is close enough to the main roads north and west from Reykjavík to be accessible with a very short detour - yet far enough to remain in virtually the same

natural state as when Eirík the Red and his son Leif the Lucky lived there at the end of the tenth century.

The district is on the route to the southern shore of the West Fjords, and involves only a 46 km detour from the main north-south Ring Road (plus 16 km to and from Eiríksstadir, site of Eirík the Red's farmhouse and birthplace of Leif the Lucky). It can be reached from Reykjavík by car within two hours.

Main communities in Dalasýsla are Búdardalur, which is the harbour site at the head of the fjord, and Laugar with its facilities for travellers including a hotel, camping site, swimming pool and folk museum.

*Inside the replica house.*  Photo: Helga H. Ágústsdóttir

The mighty forces of nature are at peace in Dalasýsla today, although their effect is still clear. Like all of Iceland the region was created by volcanic activity, although its three local volcanic centres, which erupted 6-8 million years ago to form basalt strata and rhyolite mountains, are long since extinct.

Geothermal springs are found at three sites: most prominently at Laugar in Sælingsdalur, now a base for travellers in the district, but also at Laugardalur and Reykjadalur. Many place names (containing the stem skóg-) show that woodland was widespread during the settlement in the 9th and 10th centuries, although this is now mainly confined to Dalir on the Fellsströnd coast. From its shores, sheltering snugly against the bay, to its rolling green uplands, Dalasýsla is a place to be at one with nature.

### Rich wildlife on the shores

Dalasýsla boasts exceptionally diverse bird life. The islands of Breidafjördur are the main breeding grounds for cormorants and shags in Iceland and it also has large puffin colonies, while the white-tailed eagle nests in the area too. Seals abound on the shores and farmers even harvested edible seaweed there in times of old. The sight of the sun setting on these magical shores is a completely unforgettable experience.

### Family-friendly

Dalasýsla is a family-friendly place to visit, combining historical and cultural attractions with the enchanting world of wildlife and nature. It's an ideal place to spend a few days away from the hustle and bustle of city life, to relax, be outdoors, discover and learn. The

*From the Leif Eiríksson Heritage Festival.*                    *Photo: Magnús Hjörleifsson*

many leisure options on offer include visits to Eirík the Red's farmhouse and the folk museum, walking and hiking, bird and seal watching and swimming in geothermally heated outdoor pools. Laxá is the best known of the district's many fine salmon and trout angling rivers, while inexpensive trout fishing is available in the lake of Haukadalsvatn and the lakes of Ljárskógar and Sólheimar.

## Walking and hiking

Fine trails for walking and hiking can be found all over Dalasýsla. A viewing dial has been set up on Mt. Klofningsfjall (384 m) with its panoramic view across the islands of Breidafjördur Bay to the adjoining shores of Snæfellsnes and Bardaströnd. Outstanding views can also be seen from many other mountains, which are 700-900 m high, such as Hólsfjall in Hördudalur, Jörfahnúkur in Haukadalur, Hrossaborg in Sælingsdalur and Hafratindur at Saurbær, the highest mountain in the district at 923 m. For a close-up view of nature, there are numerous trails in the lowlands, along riversides and into the valleys, not forgetting of course the special delights of strolling along the shores.

## Further information

*www.dalir.is*

*Then, when it was least expected, Gisli turned around and ran from the ridge up onto the crag known as Einhamar. There, he faced them and defended himself. [...] Everyone in Eyjolf's party was badly wounded, and Gisli died with so many and such great wounds that it was an amazement to all. They say that he never once backed off, and as far as anyone could see his last blow was no weaker than his first.*

(From Gisli Sursson's Saga)

## The Saga of Gísli Súrsson

One of the most valuable cultural heritages in Iceland is the old literature. The sagas describe the life and history of the Icelanders from the first settlement around 870 until 1100. Each region of Iceland has its own saga or sagas. There are three sagas that take place in the Westfjords, and the Saga of Gísli Súrsson is the most popular one. It is a story about the destiny of Thorbjorn Thorkelsson and his family. The saga is rather short but retains everything that a good story needs.

*Haukadalur valley, the home of Gísli Súrsson and his family.*    Photo: Þórir Örn Guðmundsson

*Sunset in Dýrafjördur.*

The story of Gísli is a typical outlaw story, one of drama with elements of evil, deceit and cruelty but also about love, friendship and loyalty. The saga begins in Norway in the Surnadal valley area south of Trondheim and the nearby islands, but moves to Iceland early in the story. Gísli and his family make their home in Haukadalur valley in Iceland's Westfjords. Action takes place in the western part of the Westfjords stretching all over the southern and northern fjords of the region.

Gísli's Saga is one of the better-known sagas of Iceland and is part of the curriculum in many Icelandic schools. As in most of the Icelandic sagas, many place names are today exactly the same as the places named in the saga. This saga-heritage is very much alive to those who live in the Westfjords.

## The story of Gísli's Saga

The saga begins by telling of Thorbjorn Thorkelsson's family, his wife Thora and their children Thordís, Thorkatla and Gísli. Thorbjorn's family was from the Surnadal valley in Norway and had lived there for many years. Thorbjorn ordered Gísli to defend the family's honour by killing the man who had tried to seduce his sister Thórdís. This led to many battles and in the end the family had to leave Norway. They sold everything they owned and sailed to

Iceland to make a new home. The voyage took a long time, but they decided eventually to go ashore at the mouth of Haukadalur's river, which is located on the south coast at Dýrafjordur. They bought land in the valley and built a farm.

Gísli married Audur Vésteinsdóttir, while his brother Thorkell married Asgerdur Thorbjornsdóttir. Their sister Thordís married Thorgrímur Thorsteinsson, who later became the Westfjords priest of the Old Norse religion (this was prior to the time of Christianity in Iceland). The whole family lived together in Haukadalur until Véstein became envious of other people. When Gísli heard that somebody was planning treachery against his blood brother and brother-in-law Véstein, he tried to calm things down. But Véstein was proud and decided to meet his

destiny. Finally he was killed at the farm of Hóll (Hill), which was Gísli and Audur's home. Gísli was also a very proud man and decided to get his revenge for Véstein's death, even though he knew that the murderer might have been his brother Thorkell. He could not kill his brother because that was against the code of all reputable men. Revenge was still required so Gísli decided to kill his brother-in-law and neighbour Thorgrímur. The widow Thordís, also Gísli's sister, later married Thorgrímur's brother Börkur. Thordís overheard Gísli say that he had killed Thorgrímur, and she told Börkur, who now had to revenge his brother's death. Gísli was sentenced to exile.

Gísli did not want to leave Iceland because he loved his wife Audur very much. Gísli built a house for Audur in Geirthjófsfjordur, and they lived there secretly. Börkur tried many times to kill Gísli but was unsuccessful. He then hired his uncle Eyjólfur the Grey from Otradalur valley in Arnarfjordur to do the job. Gísli moved around constantly to avoid potential killers. He searched diligently for help in getting his case retried, but nobody wanted to stand against Börkur. Gísli was in exile for 13 years but spent seven of those years with his wife Audur. He became tired of running away and decided to face the men who were looking for him. Finally Eyjólfur and 15 men found him in Geirthjófsfjordur. Gísli defended himself on a cliff called Einhamar. Gísli killed six men and fatally wounded another before he was himself killed. Every man with Eyjólfur had been wounded or killed. The saga tells that Gísli was as strong with his last

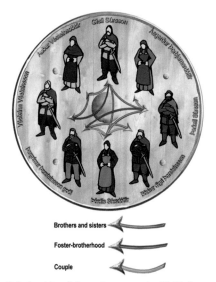

**Brothers and sisters**
**Foster-brotherhood**
**Couple**

*Relationship of the main persons in Gísli's Saga.*
*Illustration: Ómar Smári Kristinsson and Nina Ivanova*

*Signpost illustrating a part of Gísli's Saga.*

blow as with his first. Gísli's single-handed defence in this battle was remembered in Iceland as being very heroic.

*(source: Gísla Saga Súrssonar. Icelandic Old Writings. Published in 6 volumes, 1943 and reprinted 1972).*

## Tracing the Sagas in the Westfjords

It is interesting to read the saga of Gísli with a map of the Westfjords at hand. The story describes all the places so that if you were reading Gísli's Saga while travelling, you could easily find the place named or described. The place names are still the same, and some of the old paths are still well known. The names Gísli, Audur, Thorkell, Thordís and Thorgrimur are even now very common names in the Westfjords. Other place names such as Gíslasker (Gísli's-scar),

Gíslasteinn (Gísli's-boulder), Gíslagjá (Gísli's-rift) are known and used today. The names come down through the generations, even though they did not appear in Gísli's saga itself.

With both the book and map in hand it is easy to locate events and places. In Önundarfjordur for example, you can see where the old houses once stood. Véstein's house for example was located near a mountain named Hestur. You can see the farm called Holt and its meadow, where Thorvaldur's workers fought with their scythes. On the hilltop called Arnkel, the fastest horses in the fjord collapsed. Véstein's men awaited Gísli´s workers at Gemlufall, at the place where all the water begins to fall to Dýrafjordur. This place marks the point in the saga where destiny is set.

*Illustrations: Ómar Smári Kristinsson and Nína Ivanova.*

The ground seems to talk in Haukadalur when you are walking through the valley. All the old place names and landmarks are still there. The river in Haukadalur, where Gísli's Saga began, still runs there, and maps mark the location of the former farms Sæból, Hóll, Annmarkastaðir, Orrastaðir, Nefstaðir and Saltnes.

Further south in the deserted fjord Geirthjófsfjordur, you will find Audarbæ (Audur's house) and Einhamar. From Geirthjófsfjordur you can look over to Otradalur, where Eyjólfur the Grey lived. He was the one who accepted silver for killing Gísli.

Still there are other places of interest. Gestur Oddleifsson from the farm Haga at the Bardastrond coastline had second-sight and was thought to be one of the wisest men of his time. His mother Thorgerdur lived at Vadli, which is also at Bardastrond. At the farm Hvammur nearby, Thorkell Súrsson lived after he moved from Haukadalur.

Some kilometres to the east, from Hjardarnes, you have a good view of Hergil's island where Gísli's cousin Ingjaldur lived. He helped Gísli to hide from Börkur, even though he knew he was risking his own life. He told Börkur that his own reputation was spotted so it did not make any difference. The slave Bothildur rowed a boat through the strait between the shore and Hergil's island, where Gísli was hiding, in order to save his life. A little further east is the farm Audhaugur where Refur (Fox) lived. He helped Gísli more than anyone else to escape from Börkur, by hiding him in his own straw-filled bed while his wife was lying in it. Further east in Thorskafjordur (Cod fjord) the sons of Véstein took revenge for their father when they killed Thorkell Súrsson.

## The West Vikings

The value of the cultural heritage of Gísli's Saga has been realised, and the saga has been taught in elementary schools in Iceland for more than 30 years. It has also been translated into several languages. The idea of using the saga and make it visible in the region was born. The Regional Development Agency of the Westfjords initiated a development process which included research on how to use the saga for future regional development. Many ideas were generated and a regional group, which calls itself the West

*The festival place in Thingeyri .*

*Photo: Steinar R. Jónasson*

Vikings, was established in the village Thingeyri. The main objective is to find effective ways to help people remember the story and relive the events that took place.

The following projects have been completed or are in progress:

1. *Establishment of a saga trail with signposts along the road and at the most important saga sites. The saga is represented with both words and pictures.*

2. *Creation of a festival location and a Viking site built in the traditional turf style by the West Vikings. The festival location was first used in the summer of 2004, and construction continues. More than 300 people can be seated in the circle, and a big stage offers the necessary framework for all kind of events. A large hearth in the middle of the circle offers a good atmosphere for story telling, singing and gathering. A market place will be added to the area as* well as a Viking playground and eventually a longhouse.

3. *A big effort has been made to involve the local population. Different craft courses have been held, and more than 10% of the village's people own their own Viking clothes. Many children are involved and will take part in all kinds of events in the future.*

4. *A play about Gísli has been written and is performed on request in either Icelandic or English.*

5. *A West Viking offers guided tours to the Haukadalur valley.*

Future development continues and more activities and tours are planned. Eventually a Viking ship will be added. The project's ongoing development can be followed at its homepage *www.westvikings.info*

## Current environment

The Westfjords is the most remote area of Iceland and probably the most exciting. Virtually separated from the rest of Iceland, this region has remained in many ways a world apart. The Westfjords is sparsely populated, and the nature here is the same as it was a hundred years ago. Nature's silence is most impressive for many travellers visiting the Westfjords. Majestic mountains, deep blue fjords, seals, millions of birds, crisp fresh air-all of these attributes are characteristic. Farms in the Westfjords are widely scattered, and the local people have a deep understanding of their environment.

Most of Gísli´s saga takes place in Dýrafjordur. There you can find ruins from the time of Gísli´s saga. Dýrafjordur, one of the most beautiful fjords in Iceland, is surrounded by high mountains which ice age glaciers left behind when they cut valleys between the majestic mountain tops. To the north of the fjord you can see the the typical mountains of the Westfjords which are flat on top with very steep scree sides. Vegetation clings to the thin soil and reaches far up on the hillsides. On the western side of the fjord are the farm Alvidra, known since settlement times, and the ancient manor and church site Núpur. The botanical garden Skrúður near Núpur has proved that plants from much warmer climatic areas can grow in the far north. The bottom of the fjord is an untouched natural paradise. The remains of birch and mountain ash forests found are similar to the forests that were growing in Iceland at the time of the first settlement.

The village Thingeyri is situated on the south side of the fjord. The name Thingeyri comes from the Dýrafjordur-"thing" which

*West Vikings at the festival place .*                    Photo: Steinar R. Jónasson

*Shoe making seminar in Thingeyri.*
Photo: Dorothee Lubecki

indoor swimming pool is beside the camping area, which is situated close to the beach.

The mountains near Thingeyri, between Dýrafjordur and Arnarfjordur, are unlike most others in the Westfjords with impressive peaks instead of flat plateaus. They are sometimes referred to as the Westfjords Alps. Kaldbakur, the highest mountain in the Westfjords, is probably the most imposing among them, two meters short of being 1000 meters high. Under Kaldbakur rests Haukadalur valley where Gísli Súrsson lived until exiled. The route from Haukadalur to Arnarfjordur, passing the beautiful located Svalvogur lighthouse, is very challenging and exiting because of its high steep cliffs on one side and sea beaten rock beach on the other. Following this route is only recommended for jeeps with 4-wheel drive, and the actual road conditions need to be checked before driving.

was moved from a place called Valseyri to Thingeyri around the year 1000. At this regional meeting place common decisions were made. There you can see ancient relics that are today preserved by the National Relics Association.

Thingeyri is one of the oldest commercial towns in Iceland. A church has been in Thingeyri since 1911 and was designed by one of Iceland's first government architects.

The old smithy from 1913 is a special place of interest in Thingeyri. Nothing has changed. The smithy is a good example of craftmanship from the early twentieth century. All general services are available in Thingeyri, and many craftsmen live there. An

One of the numerous places of interest in the area is Hrafnseyri. The small museum and reconstructed farmhouse at Hrafnseyri in Arnarfjordur is important to all Icelanders. Jón Sigurðsson was born there in 1811. He spent most of his life in Copenhagen and spearheaded the fight for Iceland's independence.

At the bottom of the fjord Arnarfjordur is a cove called Dynjandi where beautiful waterfalls can be seen and explored. The prettiest is called Fjallfoss. A camping site is situated in this cove.

On the way south, following the mountain road Dynjandisheidi, Geirthjófsfjordur appears on the right hand

*Young West Vikings .*

*Photo: Steinar R. Jónasson*

side. It has been deserted since 1960 and is one of the few fjords in the Westfjords that has not been affected by modern day farming or road construction. A slightly difficult walk down into the fjord leads to the peaceful birch forest where Audur, Gísli´s wife, lived and hid him until he was killed.

In the Westfjords you will travel through the whole range of Icelandic flora, from the shore and meadows, through birch and willow, to mossy moors. On a stroll among driftwood on the shore one can see birds, seals and an occasional arctic fox. Residents from this area are known for their hospitality and helpfulness to travellers.

## Further information
*www.vestfirdir.is*
*www.vesturferdir.is*

*Grettir led the ox, which walked very stiffly because it was tethered and rather fat. The ox grew exhausted, and when it got as far as Tittlingastadir it could not go any further. [...] they saw a man walking towards them with an ox on his back: it was Grettir carrying the ox. Everyone was astonished at what he was capable of.*

(From the Saga of Grettir the strong)

## The Saga of Grettir

He has been called the Last Viking, born on the cusp of Paganism and Christianity in the northern part of Iceland. An outcast, a fighter - a loner who was stronger than anyone around and had nothing in common with his contemporaries.

The turbulent life of Grettir Ásmundarson is recounted in the famous *Saga of Grettir*, which take place mostly in the Húnathing region of north Iceland.

Húnathing is a large and grassy county in the west of northern Iceland, which extends from Skagatá in the north down into the

*Visitors at the 2004 Grettir Festival: A group of Faeroese dancers by the plaque commemorating Grettir's mother, Ásdís. The plaque is located at Bjarg in Midfjördur fjord.*                    Photo: Karl Sigurgeirsson

central highlands. It is an agricultural region, while various services (light industry and tourism) have been developing in recent years. Húnathing has three centres of population, at Hvammstangi, Blönduós and Skagaströnd. The fisheries have long played an important role in the local economy, and in olden times there were boats all along the coast, and various peripheral resources were well utilised: seal and shark were hunted, down was gathered from the nests of the eider duck, and driftwood was the only source of timber. Sheep graze on the inland heaths, where large lakes and rivers abound in trout and salmon. This well-vegetated region offers the visitor a variety of landscape and outdoor activities.

Iceland was settled in the late 9th and early 10th century, mainly from Norway.

Within a few decades people had settled all over the country, including Húnathing.

The settlement in Húnathing flourished and "heroes rode through the countryside," as the Icelandic sagas say - many of which are set in Húnathing. The best known is the local sagas is certainly the *Saga of Grettir*, while others include the *Saga of the People of Vatnsdalur*, the *Saga of the Sworn Brothers*, the *Saga of the Confederates* and the *Saga of the Slayings on the Heath*, etc. They are set largely within the Húnathing area, and were probably written locally, perhaps at the Thingeyrar monastery.

The settlers of Iceland were Vikings and their descendants: adventurers who undertook the perilous sea voyage across the ocean to an unknown island.

*The annual Grettir Festival is held at Grettir's birthplace, Bjarg. Each year the festival draws large crowds of guests, both local residents and tourists.*

Photo: Karl Sigurgeirsson

The *Saga of Grettir* is believed have been written in the early 14th century (1320-50). Grettir himself is mentioned by many older sources, always as a well-known character. Whoever wrote down the *Saga of Grettir* must have relied on many oral sources.

The *Saga of Grettir* has survived in copies written on vellum, the oldest from the last quarter of the 15th century, as well as in numerous paper manuscripts. The large number of manuscripts gives a strong clue to the saga's popularity over the centuries. Twenty-seven manuscripts survive from the 17th century, and 21 from the 18th. Two of the latter manuscripts contain full-page illustrations of Grettir: *AM 426 folio* has a picture from the late 17th century, and *Lbs 203 folio* contains another, by an unknown artist, from around 1753. In that same folio we also see an illustration of Ásmundur Greyhair, Grettir's father.

The *Saga of Grettir* tells of Grettir's conflicts and confrontations with both natural and supernatural enemies in Iceland and Norway, and part of the story focuses on his travels in Norway. Grettir spent 19 years in exile, longer than anyone else in Icelandic history, and was finally killed on Drangey island in Skagafjördur. The *Saga of Grettir* has been published in numerous languages and is well known in Europe. In Germany, plays based on the *Saga of Grettir* have been written and performed; Grettir is the subject of poems composed in the Faroe Islands; and on the Scottish islands of Shetland the story of Grettir the Strong has been told by storytellers for generations. The *Saga of*

*Through the years, The Saga of Grettir has been an inspiration to artists and authors alike. Drawing by artist Halldór Pétursson*

*Grettir* is a hero-centred story bearing many of the characteristics of a good novel: introduction, climax, and dénouement. It is nonetheless clear that the story is based on real-life events and people who lived in Iceland around the year 1000.

The farm of Bjarg in Midfjördur is the central location of the *Saga of Grettir*. Grettir was born and brought up there, and his various childhood pranks and adventures are recounted in the saga. He was a wild and uncontrollable lad, and his destiny was clear from an early age. The visitor to Bjarg today can see a number of features that relate to Grettir and the saga. Grettir, who was hugely strong, is said to have played with large rocks at Bjarg known as *Grettistök* (Grettir's Grasp), which visitors attempt to lift to test their strength. Kirkjuhóll (Church Hill) is

*Grettir lived on the island of Drangey in Skagafjördur fjord for the last three years of his life. It was here that his enemies managed to vanquish him with the aid of sorcery.*    Photo: Pétur Ingi Björnsson

where Grettir's father built a church, and the site of the farmhouse in saga times has been identified. Under a large boulder, Grettistþúfa (Grettir's Hummock), Grettir's head is buried. A monument has been erected on the farm to Ásdís, Grettir's mother.

Facilities for visitors are good at Bjarg, with information panels and marked footpaths. Visitors can visit the farm to learn about Grettir; in summer a guide is available every Sunday in June, July and August, to tell visitors about the *Saga of Grettir* and this heritage site.

Many more places in Húnathing play a part in the *Saga of Grettir*: ball-games are described at Midfjardarvatn lake, and Grettir takes part in a horse-fight at Langafit, adjacent to the village of Laugarbakki. At Hrútafjardarháls, another large rock may be seen, on which Grettir tried his strength as he lay in wait for his enemies. At the Arnarvatn lake in the highlands, Grettir spent three winters when he was an outlaw in

*An unforgettable event at the Grettir Festival is the "strong man (and woman)" competition for the prized Grettir Cup.*                    Photo: Karl Sigurgeirsson

Iceland, and various placenames recall his presence. There are also remnants of shacks where he is said to have resided. The highland lakes are remote, and abound in fish, so it was easy for Grettir to survive there. A crucial turning-point in the saga is Grettir's fight with the ghost Glámur at Thórhallastadir in Vatnsdalur; after he defeated Glámur, the ghost's eyes always haunted him, and he could not be alone after dark. It was after this battle that things began to go wrong for Grettir. The ruins of the old farmstead at Thórhallastadir are still visible.

Grettir wandered widely in north and west Iceland during his 19 years of outlawry. At Reyhólar in west Iceland, for instance, is Grettislaug (Grettir's Pool), where Grettir bathed. In Skagafjörður, the next county to Húnaþing, is another Grettir's Pool, which is mentioned in the saga. Grettir spent the last three years of his life on the offshore island of Drangey in Skagafjörður, with his brother Illugi. On one occasion Grettir swam ashore from the island to fetch embers, after the brothers' fire had gone out; he bathed in Grettir's Pool when he came ashore. Grettir

*One of many Grettistak (Grettir's Grasp) in Iceland.*                    Photo: Pétur Jónsson

was under constant attack from his enemies, who finally defeated him on the island of Drangey, with the help of magic.

No human was Grettir's equal, but he could not overcome the supernatural. On Drangey traces of the buildings where Grettir and Illugi lived can still be seen.

## Grettistak

Though Grettir himself is no longer with us, his story lives on in print and in people's minds. Many places in Iceland, including a number of well-known historical sites, are named after him, many of them in West Húnathing. In many places around the country, there are huge rocks known as *Grettistök* (Grettir's Grasp), which Grettir is reputed to have lifted to try his strength. Several of these are mentioned in the *Saga of Grettir*.

In 2002, a private non-profit making organisation called *Grettistak* was founded in West Hunathing. *Grettistak* focuses on the culture and history of the county, with particular emphasis on the *Saga of Grettir*. Its objective is to make the *Saga of Grettir*, and other local stories of historical significance, visible and accessible to tourists and local citizens alike and to use these stories to attract a greater number of tourists to the area, with the long-term aim of promoting all types of services and contributing to the development of the region as a whole.

The establishment of a special information centre on the *Saga of Grettir* has started. Since 1997 an annual Grettir Festival has been held; it is a family-oriented affair, with a variety of entertainment. A guided tour of Grettir's birthplace and childhood home is available, and guests can learn about the various placenames and historical sites in the area and hear the highlights of Grettir's life and saga. A feature of the festival is the contest for the Grettir Cup, for which men and women compete in tests of strength. There are also games for children. The festival ends with song and dance, and the chanting of rímur, traditional Icelandic verses.

The Húnathing region offers a wide variety of places of interest: spectacular scenery and natural history, historical sites and relics of Icelandic heritage. Tourism is expanding in the region, and visitors are warmly welcomed.

## Further reading

- *The Saga of Grettir the Strong,* trans. Bernard Scudder, Penguin 2005
- *Three Icelandic Outlaw Sagas,* trans. Anthony Faulkes and George Johnston, Everyman 2001.
- *Grettir's saga*, transl. Denton Fox & Hermann Pálsson, University of Toronto Press 1974.
- R. J. Glendinning: *Grettis Saga and European Literature in the Late Middle Ages.* Mosaic IV (1970-71) 49-61.
- K. Grimstad: *A Comic Role of the Viking in the Family Sagas.* Studies for Einar Haugen (1972) 243-52.

## Further information

*www.grettistak.is*
*www.northwest.is*

*Gunnar Hamundarson [...] was big and strong and an excellent fighter. He could swing a sword and throw a spear with either hand, if he wished, and he was so swift with a sword that there seemed to be three in the air at once. He could shoot with a bow better than anyone else, and he always hit what he aimed at. He could jump higher than his own height, in full fighting gear, and just as far backward as forward.*

(From Njal's Saga)

# Njál's Saga, the Queen of the Sagas, South Iceland

W hat happens if you step into the world of the Icelandic sagas? The sagas are virtually an entire universe, complete with the characters, events, and history of the Viking Age in Iceland and nearby countries. The world of the sagas is populated with heroes who made their mark on their surroundings and their times, and with warriors who travelled by land and by sea, living their adventures and battling against earls and kings.

The Icelandic sagas were written in the 13th and 14th centuries and are based on a number of historical events. Their greatest strength, however, lies in the way in which they were written, in the narrative style and the rich characterization that draw the reader and the hearer into a fascinating world where values are different than those reigning today. The longest is Njála - Njál's Saga - which has often been called the Queen of the Sagas.

*The wiew to glacier Eyjafjallajokull, from Gunnar's home at Hlidarendi.*   Photo: Sigrún R. Ragnarsdóttir

*Many of the manuscripts were written by christian munks in the late Middle Ages.*
Photo: Tobias Klose

pencraft, the making of ink, and the technology related to book-making in the era.

To complement the history portrayed on the walls of the exhibition hall, employees recount the saga for guests, adding anecdotes from the wellspring of mythology and other knowledge of history and Mediaeval thought as these are known in Iceland.

Most of the historical locations from Njála are well known, and a large number of them have been marked with signs already so that those wishing to acquaint themselves with the story can follow its path. In addition, the museum's employees and a number of local residents have specialized in guiding interested tourists around these historical surroundings while recounting the part of the saga that is appropriate to each location.

Njála tells of the close friendship between the hero, Gunnar of Hlídarendi, and the sage, Njáll of Bergthórshvoll; and it tells of their wives, who are sworn enemies and think nothing of sacrificing the lives of slaves and labourers in the service of their own virulent disputes. At the Historical Museum in the South Iceland town of Hvolsvöllur is an exhibition that tells the story of the main characters in this timeless book. Other aspects of these bygone times are treated as well: the voyages of Scandinavians and Icelanders, the ships of the day and the conquests made, the impetus to create written stories, the development of Mediaeval

The Historical Museum boasts a Viking Hall where groups of guests may eat a delicious meal with grilled mutton as the centrepiece, followed by the house's own special entertainment. This offerings include a programme where local residents recount selected parts of the sagas in word and in song, with piano accompaniment. Several of the local people are well-trained singers, and they have engaged the assistance of an accompanist and a story teller who are also from the area. Texts available in PowerPoint format makes it possible for the guests to read the texts to the songs in English and/or German, even though the singers perform in Icelandic.

*Mount Thrihyrning and Mount Hekla in the surroundings of Njál's Saga.*     Photo: Sigrún R. Ragnarsdóttir

On other occasions, people come from nearby areas and perform a comedy about the saga, and sometimes an accordion player from the district plays at the tables.

Great stress is placed on the participation of local residents in this entertainment and in the narrative that the museum considers as one of its roles.

During the summer, the museum has held a series of lecture-meetings in collaboration with local people who invite equestrians on tours of the Trail of Njála. The lecture series has been entitled "Njála with Sunday coffee." Every Sunday scholars, politicians, and members of the press have discussed specific aspects of the saga and their interpretation. Response has been overwhelmingly positive, and guests have even come all the way from the capital, Reykjavík, solely to listen to the lectures and participate in the discussions taking place afterward.

All of these activities are designed to enhance the role of history in the minds of local people and other Icelanders. The realm that the guest enters is utterly unlike the everyday realities of modern life. In the world of Mediaeval times - the Viking Age - the guest partakes of an exciting and mysterious existence where fixed rules, constant tradition, and dignity and honour play an important role. The world of the Viking Age is enchanting and exhilarating, and there is every reason to make a supreme effort to render it accessible and intelligible to the people of today.

**Further information**
*www.njala.is*
*www.southiceland.is*

*Thjórsárdalur valley was the site of a flourishing Settlement Age community that was later abandoned and then disappeared under ash in 1104, when the volcano Mount Hekla erupted for the first time in the history of Iceland. While some 40 archaeological relics are registered in the valley, it is expected that further work will reveal an even greater number of findings.*

## The settlers in the area

Iceland's most popular tourist area, the Árnessýsla county upcountry boasts a wealth of natural wonders and well-marked historic sites. Hot springs and geothermal heat characterise the region and make their impact on the culture of the area, as well as on the historical sites marking milestones in the history of the land and society of Iceland. The Árnes uplands stretch from Thingvellir to the Thjórsá River and into the central highlands. Its inhabitants number some 2,500 and populate four municipalities.

In Landnámabók (the Book of Settlement) it is stated that Thorbjörn Laxakarl was the first settler in the Gnúpverjahreppur district, where he built the farm at Hagi. Ketilbjörn the Old settled both the Biskupstungur area and Grímsnes and established a farm named Mosfell. Two

*Iceland was settled from 874-930, largely by proud farmers seeking freedom from the tyranny of King Harald Fair-hair of Norway.*

Photo: ÁA

brothers named Már and Bröndólfur Naddoddsson settled Hrunamannahreppur district. Ólafur "Shaggy-Brows" sailed from Lofoten in Norway, settled Skeid, and then made his home at Ólafsvellir. One of the chief manors in South Iceland, Ólafsvellir was the site of a church built in early Christian times. The church currently standing there dates from 1897. Áshildarmýri, named after Ólafur Shaggy-Brows' wife Áshildur, was an ancient meeting place in the vicinity of Skeid, where local farmers met to express their vigorous opposition to foreign domination and oppression.

## Thjórsárdalur valley

Thjórsárdalur valley was the site of a flourishing Settlement Age community that was later abandoned and then disappeared under pumice in 1104, when the volcano Mount Hekla erupted for the first time in the history of Iceland. While some 40 archaeological relics are registered in the valley, it is expected that further work will reveal an even greater number of findings. A great deal of ironworking took place in Thjórsárdalur valley, and slag and charcoal have been found all over the area. Some of

*From the Settlement day June 2004.*  *Photo: ÁA*

*The settlement farm at Stöng. The ruins are preserved under the red roof.*  *Photo: ÁA*

*Gjáin, a miniature sample of Icelandic nature, beautiful lava formations, caves and waterfalls. Only 10 minutes walk from the excavated ruins at Stöng.*

Photo: ÁA

these relics have been studied by scholars. The first research work was carried out in the 19th century, while the most recent studies date from the year 2001. The best known of these are the archaeological excavations in 1939, when Nordic archaeologists studied six farms and a cemetery in Thjórsárdalur valley. Among the settlements studied was the farmstead at Stöng. The 1939 research represented a watershed because it marked the beginning of geologist Dr. Sigurdur Thórarinsson's study of tephrochronology. This period in archaeological research also saw the beginning of pollen analysis and the osteological studies on skeletons from ancient times.

When it was decided to build a replica of a Commonwealth Era farmstead in 1974, in commemoration of the 1,100-year anniversary of Iceland's settlement, the ruins of the farm at Stöng were used as a model for the construction of the hypothetical manor.

Stöng consists of a large hall, a living room, a byre and a house which has been identified as a toilet by some archaeologists. Some outhouses, a cow shed and a smithy, were also excavated. The remains have been dated to the early 12th century. A later research during the 1980's and 1990's revealed a church with some graves.

The Stöng ruin was the first one in Iceland to be made accessible for tourists.

Just after the excavation a house was constructed to cover the ruins and the turf walls were reconstructed on top of the stone foundations which were discovered when the site was excavated.

The only Stöng resident who is known by name was a man called Gaukur Trandilsson, about whom there was once a saga that is now lost. He and the mistress of Steinastadir enjoyed a relationship of particular warmth, as is revealed in the following dance verse:
*Gaukur lived at Stöng in days of yore'n'*
*the path to Steinastadir was short'n'well worn.*

*Visitors from Lofoten, Norway by Hjálparfoss waterfall, in Thjórsárdalur valley.*  Photo: ÁA

**Gjáin**
The canyon called Gjáin in Thjórsárdalur valley boasts spellbinding natural beauty characterised by grassy hills, rivulets, water-

*Skálholt was the focus of Icelandic history and culture for centuries until the bishopric was moved to Reykjavik around 1800.*  Photo: ÁA

falls, mountain springs, and caves. According to legend, Gaukur at Stöng chose this place for his trysts with his paramour, Thurídur of Steinastadir.

## Skálholt

Skálholt is an ancient manor farm and bishopric whose history dates back to the year 1056. For centuries the school that was operated there, Skálholtsskóli, was the leading educational institution in Iceland. Skálholt occupies a position of well-deserved dominance in the history of Mediaeval

Icelandic books and manuscripts, for it was there that the books and manuscripts currently found in library collections were written and preserved.

## Thingvellir

Now a protected historical site, Thingvellir is revered in the hearts and minds of Icelanders. It was the site of the founding of Althingi, the Parliament of Iceland, in the year 930, and a great number of the most remarkable events in Icelandic history occurred there. Designated as a UNESCO World Heritage

*Þingvellir National Park. Two severe earthquakes occurred in South Iceland in the summer of 2000. The earthquakes were a result of movement of the Eurasian and N- American plate boundaries that run through Iceland. At Þingvellir the plates break apart and the land between subsides.* Photo: Rafn Hafnfjörð

*Strokkur, located nearby the famous Geysir gives a performance every few minutes, shooting a tower of water and steam 30 meters into the air.* Photo: Rögnvaldur Guðmundsson

Site in the year 2004, the Thingvellir National Park is among some 800 sites of cultural and natural significance that are considered to have unique value on a global scale.

## Geysir

Doubtless the best-known geyser in the world, Geysir has lent its name to the English language in order to christen the phenomenon of the periodically spouting hot spring. Historical sources back to the 13th century mention Geysir, whose activity has varied through time and often changes as a result of earthquakes. When Geysir was at its most active, its eruptions spouted scalding geothermal water streams some 60 - 80 m into the air.

## Gullfoss, the Golden Falls

The canyon below Gullfoss extends for some 2,5 kilometres and reaches a depth of 70 metres.  For thousands of years the river has followed its coarse delighting   tourists with beauty and power.

Sigridur Tómasdóttir the farmer's daughter in Bratholt by Gullfoss was born 1871.  She often accompanied visitors to Gullfoss,  many of whom had travelled great distances to catch sight of it.  At the turn of the 19th century efforts began to acquire the rights to waterfalls in Iceland for industrial and hydroelectric purposes, often by agents for foreign enterprises.  When Gullfoss came into the possession of such agents Sigridur, rose up to fight against several of the most

*Gullfoss falls 32 meters in two stages.*    Photo: ÁÁ

powerful men in Iceland. A monument to Sigríður was erected there in 1978.

## Further information

*www.sveitir.is*
*www.thingvellir.is*
*www.skalholt.is*
*www.geysircenter.com*

*Eirik was reluctant to give up his faith but Thjodhild was quick to convert and had a church built a fair distance from the house. It was called Thjodhild's church and there she prayed, along with those other people who converted to Christianity, of whom there were many. After her conversion, Thjodhild refused to sleep with Eirik, much to his displeasure.*

(From Eirik the Red's Saga)

## A visit to The Great Palaarsuaq - Eric the Red[1]

A little more than a 1000 years ago the Vikings arrived in the south of Greenland. In the sagas we find many stories of how it took place. We are told about the settler, the bellicose Eric the Red, who travelled from Iceland to Greenland and spent three years looking for a good place to settle. To him the southern part of Greenland must have appeared like paradise on earth! Lots of vegetation, wide and flat areas, warm summer temperatures - as well as hills where livestock could graze at an even higher altitude than back in Iceland. The manor was built at Brattahlid - today Qassiarsuk. Actually he may have settled in

*Tunulliarfik Fiord, South Greenland.*

Photo: Agne Säterberg

Narsaq to begin with, because it is here we find the oldest dated Norse farm, but the first church was definitely built at Brattahlid.

For this we can thank Tjodhilde, Eric's wife. She was a strong-minded woman who did not let anyone tell her what to do - not even her husband - and she carried her plan through. It is hardly likely that anyone else could have won over Eric!

## A portrait of Eric the Red

Eric was known back in Iceland as well as in Greenland as a stubborn mule, not easily moved, and insisting on his right to do wrong - including the use of violence - should he feel like it. He was most definitely not a model of virtue, so why do we still remember all these stories? It may be due to the fact that they entail some of the same

kind of fascination as all stories about strong men in the wilderness and the tough ones that survived. He - like many others of his time and place - must have been immensely strong and resilient. It is difficult even to imagine the kind of hardship he must have suffered during his first years in Greenland.

Eric the Red was a real hotheaded, red-blooded type of man. The fact that the following generation was also very adventurous does not diminish the story - Leif the Lucky discovered a whole new continent.

The sagas only narrate the history of the first few generations of settlers in Greenland - peasants are not nearly as exciting as wild Vikings. But Eric, Tjodhilde and Leif still stand out, and they lived in what is now the municipality of Narsaq. We point out the

*Reconstruction of Thodhilde's Church, Qassiarsuk (Brattahlid).*    Photo: Narsaq Museum

places and maybe shiver a little. This is actually where they lived!

His contemporaries did not consider Eric the Red neither a hero nor an idol. He was - in short - a hothead with a murderous temper, and in fact two countries outlawed him. After having fled to Iceland he did not stand out as a large farmer or any kind of top-notch. He was referred to a barren and poor corner of the new country and had great trouble supporting his growing family.

Due to his rather inflated ego he was not very comfortable with his socially low standing in Iceland. On the other hand he must have been very pleased ending up as a chief in a new country named by him.

Was he a good father and husband? Well - he certainly was rather fond of his wife Tjodhilde and as a "real man" he probably was a role model for their three sons.  But he was not faithful to his wife, and fathered a daughter out of wedlock - the horrible Freydis, who in the sagas is depicted as thoroughly bad - in contrast to her brothers Leif, Thorvald and Thorstein, who are all depicted as "good guys".

Eric was a strong character, who did not allow himself to be affected by anything - apart from two exceptions. The sagas tell us how deeply wounded he was, when Tjodhilde refused to sleep with him as a consequence of the arguments they had concerning her interest in the new religion - Christianity - and her desire to be christened. Eric was a convinced heathen.

The other fact, which, according to sagas, really bothered him, was a time, when he was hosting a yuletide party, and they ran out of mead. This was a man who had his priorities in order!

## Who came first?

It is probably true that Eric ended his days as a respected chief of the small settlements of the far-away Norse Greenland. But he is certainly not looked upon as a hero in contemporary Greenland - today he is considered an annoyance more than anything else!

This is probably due to the fact that the period around the first millennium was also when the first Inuit of the Thule-culture began their wanderings across the Ellesmere Island (Baffin Island) and on to Greenland. Without knowing one another two waves of immigrants were arriving at the West Coast - one from the South and one from the North. But then they were to meet - probably in the Northwest of Greenland sometime around the 12th Century.

This is not the place to explain the rest of the story, but without remittance one question is always asked: *Who was there first?*

Politically speaking the question is of no relevance, as the Norsemen have long perished. But this does not alter the fact, that in contemporary Greenland there are people who are not happy to ascertain the fact, that actually Eric the Red was the first man to settle at what one thousand years later would

*Christian Motzfeldt, milking his cow in on the sheepfarm in Timerliit, South Greenland.*
Photo: Kate Kärrberg

be known as the municipality of Narsaq, and that this landnam probably took place a little less than a hundred years *prior* to the first *Inuit* - the forefathers of the present Greenlanders - crossing Ellesmere Island to the Avanersuaq of today. But in fact the Norsemen were the earliest settlers.

The self-evident solution to this "problem" is of course that Greenland - just as any other nation - has been subjected to the comings and goings of people through hundreds and thousands of years interspersed with long intervals without settlers. Neither the Norsemen nor the Inuit of the Thule Culture were the first settlers in this area, and in the sagas we are told that  Eric the Red and his people encountered ruins as well as remnants from earlier inhabitants, when they arrived in Greenland.

The question remains whether our  - the Greenlanders of today - genetic build-up contains traces of these long-forgotten people, whoever they may have been, including the Norsemen. A fascinating question, but alas too circumstantial in this context!

## The paths of culture

What the sagas do not tell us about the settlers, but which we never the less know, is not the least exciting part of the story. The kind of life the Norsemen lead as farmers is not less impressive. At that time - as well as today - it took a large amount of perseverance, stubbornness and industry to make a living from farming. Unfortunately they were so stubborn, that in the end they died. They succumbed to a change in climate, and we still do not know precisely why. But in reality they probably were rather *"palaasuarq-like"!*

The Norse scene is placed in southern Greenland. The landscape they travelled across, distances, which appear endless, the remains of their buildings. In fact we know of more than 400 registered Norse ruins, some of which are large and famous tourist sites such as Brattahlid, Gardar and Hvalsey, while others remain unknown to most people. For example who knows of the church at Dyrnæs (just outside Narsaq), the bishop's farm behind Sissarluttoq in Igalikup Kangerlua or the nunnery next to the hot springs of Unaartoq. They - and many others - are all worth visiting, even though the large distances make it difficult.

*Landnam manor, dwelling house, Narsaq.*                    *Photo: Narsaq Museum*

Narsaq is a good starting-point for a cultural tour. We begin at the landnam-manor down by the harbour in the town of Narsaq. Amongst all the Norse ruins of Greenland this is absolutely unique in as much as we here have an example from the earliest part of the Norse period. The results of a carbon-14 analysis place it around the year 1000 AD. In other words this is from the same period as the remains of the original foundations of the Tjodhilde church, which today are hidden below a marking in the shape of a peaty wall just across from the church at Qassiarsuk. The only certified early Norse ruin, which still remains visible to the naked eye, is the one in Narsaq. At this site archaeologist have also discovered a number of artefacts, which either due to shape and/or ornaments may be referred to the Viking period.

In the dwelling house of the farm one can trace the remains of at least two construction periods, and not only age but also a very well preserved system of stone built channels carrying water supplies into the house as well as transporting sewage, make this an outstanding Norse ruin.

The building is very valuable, both as a visible Norse ruin, but also because it contains a whole lot of information about the Norse farms in general. It was however a rather confusing sight, that met the visitor following the first excavations during the 1950ies, and nor was the entrance from behind the sheep slaughtering house very inviting. It was therefore decided by the museum in Narsaq to restore the ruins of what must be said to be an important asset to the town.

*Viking face. Original Norse artefact, Narsaq Museum.*            Photo: Narsaq Museum

Restoration work has been carried out thanks to funding from the *EU's Northern Periphery Programme*. It was completed in 2005 by the construction of a number of footpaths and a platform with information boards. This is supplemented by the publication of a number of leaflets, available locally and by a multi-lingual homepage with information available for those, who wish to seek information beforehand, and it contains a number of relevant links to different Viking websites of the North Atlantic area.

But this is not all. In close proximity to the ruin area we will build a Norse Information Centre (2006-2007) where original artefacts form the landnam manor will be exhibited along with spectacular reconstructions in a contemporary see-touch-feel kind of exhibition aimed at adults as well as children. The centre will also include a café and a museum shop. Our aim is to create an interesting site for the visiting tourist as well as much-needed employment for the locals.

After Narsaq the history of Southern Greenland will act as a guide to the cultural landscape of the area. One has to actively cross the land along the fjords - following the paths of our ancestors. They - Inuit as well as Norsemen - have left traces almost everywhere in this magnificent landscape, and there is no lack of places of interest. One will here find a possibility of immersion into a different world, which many modern city-dwellers will travel far to find. One will also have the possibility of introspection - of exploring ones innermost thoughts like a

*Visitors at archeological site.* Photo: Narsaq Museum

kind of pilgrim; many themes may be presented as markers on a cultural tour. In fact the possibilities are manifold.

## Qassiarsuk (Brattahlid)

The obvious place to visit after Narsaq is Qassiarsuk (Brattahlid). The two reconstructions, Tjodhilde's church and the long house of Eric the Red are placed alongside the original ruins. Thus one feels the varied "true" past as well as being able to experience the historical dimension by entering a (more or less) complete building from that period.

The Norse reconstructions at Qassiarsuk were presented to the municipality of Narsaq and the Gardar Foundation during the anniversary in 2000. So far the buildings are empty, but work is carried out in order to make them "alive".

In order to do so a number of possibilities have to be considered and it is necessary to obtain a comprehensive knowledge of similar attractions throughout the North Atlantic area. On the British Isles, in Norway, in Iceland and in New Foundland we have a number of Viking villages with rich and informative reconstructions, which are visited

*Brattahlid, present-day Qassiarsuk.*

*Photo: Narsaq Museum*

by many people - also those, who spend their free time to live as Vikings.

While working with and caring for our cultural treasures we are presently met with a new demand: A demand for good quality. We should be conscious of the uniqueness of *our* share of the Northern cultural heritage. And the answer to this demand is not simply to copy what may already be seen at other Viking sites all over the North Atlantic area. This will be the challenge confronting us in the years to come.

## Other sites

From Qassiarsuk there are a number of possible continuations of the tour - to Igaliku, to Hvalsey and further across Southern Greenland. A cultural tour is planned in order to create natural stops at the sites en route. This is true of both the places where historical events took place such as the Benedictine nunnery by the hot springs at Uunartoq and - further south - in the district of Nanortalik, the Augustinian monastery at the magnificent Tasermiut / Ketilsfjord and of the Norse Atlantic harbour for centuries, Ikigaat / Herjolfsnæss.

It is also true of areas that are still in use. Thus one may observe the remains of a medieval Norse farm, where the early inhabitants of Narsaq used to spear their fish behind stone embankments *(saputit)* - and where we today fish for the Arctic char.

*Hvalsey church ruin.*

Photo: Rögnvaldur Guðmundsson

*Entrance to the diocesan tithebarn at Gardar, present day Igaliku.*          Photo: Agne Säterberg

It's intended to direct the visitor to the hostels run by sheep farmers; the hostels will frequently be placed next to Norse ruins. Apart from accommodation these also offer the visitor a chance to taste the fare of the Norsemen such as homemade cheese and dried meat.

There are many things to be discovered if one sets out on the Viking Trail.

## Further reading
Jette Arneborg: *Saga trails - Brattahlid, Gardar, Hvalsey Fjord's church: four chieftain's farmsteads in the Norse settlement of Greenland.* Co-financed by the EU-programme NPP Interreg IIIB, Destination Viking Sagalands. Nanortalik museum,

Qaqortoq museum and Narsaq museum 2005.

Icelandic sources on Greenland:
*Book of the Icelanders,* by Ari the Learned
*Book of the Settlements*
*Tale of the Greenlanders*
*Tale of Gudmund Arason the Priest*
*Greenland Chronicle*

[1] *In Greenlandic "Palaarsuaq" means "a bad lot" or "the bad guy"*

## Further information
*www.southgreenland.gl*

*Sigmund and his fellows had now got to a rock that jutted over the sea, and could hear men's voices all round them. Then Thore said, "Let us stand at bay here, as fate will have it." "I am not fit for fighting," said Sigmund, [...] " let us therefore leap off the rock and betake us to swimming." "We will do as it pleases thee," said Thore. They took that counsel, and leapt off the cliff into the sea.*
(From the Færeyinga Saga)

# The Faroe Islands and the Færeyinga Saga

Far out in the mercury-shining North Atlantic Ocean there lies a lonely lead coloured land, the Faroe Islands. Northwest of the Shetland Islands, between Norway and Iceland, the 18 islands make up a complete little society with its friendly people and great natural beauty. There you can see blue mountains, grass green valleys, firths and sounds with strong currents and fierce tides. In some places the shore is steep with cliffs crowded with seabirds and in some places flat and sandy. The colourful villages nestle by the bays and inlets, and in the middle of all lies the capital, Tórshavn with its 18,000 inhabitants. The people, about 48,000 in all, talk their own nordic language, have their own flag, and the old lawthing, løgting. A strong and deep history lives in Faroese culture like the deep blue sea that surrounds the islands.

*The view from the top of Skúvoy with Stóra Dímun and Lítla Dímun in the background.*
Photo: Rögnvaldur Guðmundsson

## The area of Sandoy, Skúvoy and Dímun

Ferðaráð Føroya (Faroe Islands Tourist Board) and Føroya Fornminnissavn (The National Museum of Faroe Islands) are working together with Sandoyar Sýslu Ferðalag (Tourist Organisation in Sandoy), which runs Kunningarstovuna heima á Sandi (The Tourist Information Center in Sandur) and highlights the Sagalands-project in the area of Sandoy, Skúgvoy and Dímun. The purpose of the project is to use archaeology, Færeyinga Saga and stories from the area to make its history more visible and its historical sites more attractive to tourists and as a result to strengthen and develop the cultural tourism.

"Maður er nevndur Grímur Kamban..." Grímur was the first man who settled in the Faroe Islands at the beginning of the 9th century. His grandson and great grandson were among the first settlers in Iceland at around 874. One famous family at that time was Gøtuskeggjar, they descended from Eyð the Deepminded.

*The area around Sandoy which features in the Færeyinga Saga.*

### The Færeyinga Saga

The Færeyinga Saga is a collection of various texts in the Icelandic Sagas, and describes events that took place in the Faroes in the decades before and after the year 1000 A.D. - e.g. events connected with the introduction of Christianity to the islands. In 1832 it was collected into a work of literature and published under the title Færeyinga Saga. Researchers agree that an Icelander wrote the texts around the year of 1200 AD.

Tróndur í Gøtu in Eysturoy was an intelligent but evil man. In Skúvoy and Dímun the brothers Brestir and Beinir lived, his cousins, who were chiefs that ruled over half of the islands, the chief that ruled over the other half of the islands was Havgrímur, who lived in Hovi in Suðuroy. Havgrímur and the brothers Brestir and Beinir became enemies, and Havgrímur turns to Tróndur to get help and together they attack the brothers in Dímun. In the battle both Havgrímur and the brothers Brestir and Beinir are killed. As the nine-year-old son of Brestir, Sigmundur,

*The beginning of the Færeyinga Saga in the Flateyarbók: "Maðr er nefndr grímr kamban..." (There was a man named Grim Kamban...).*

Photo: The Arni Magnusson Institute, Iceland

*The southernmost area featured in the Færeyinga Saga. View of the village of Sandur on Sandoy, looking towards the islands of Skúvoy, Stóra Dímun and Lítla Dímun, with Suðuroy in the horizon.*
Photo: S. V. Arge

and the eleven-year-old son of Beinir, Tórir, witness the killing of their fathers, Tróndur wants to have the two young boys killed, but better men, e.g. Tróndur's mother brother, Bjarni from Svínoy, prevented him from doing that.

After these killings Tróndur became chief over all of the islands, and the young boys, Sigmundur and Tórir, had to follow Tróndur to his home in Gøta. Shortly there after he sent them as slaves with a Norwegian merchant, who, when back to Norway, set them free and gave them the money, Tróndur had paid him. Sigmundur and Tórir then lived in the mountains with an outlaw called Úlvur and his family. When they after

some years left the outlawed family to visit Earl Hákon, the daughter of Úlvur, Turið, was carrying Sigmundur's child.

At the court of the earls Hákon, Sveinur and Eirikur, Sigmundur and Tórir are received by the earls, who helped them to find outfit for a viking expedition. After four years in viking, Sigmundur and Tórir decided to sail to the Faroe Islands to take revenge for their fathers. In the meantime Tróndur í Gøtu himself holds sovereignity over Brestir's and Beinir's half of the islands. Sigmundur now travels between the Faroe Islands and Norway as the earls' man on the islands. He reconciles the outlawed Úlvur with the earls, marries his daughter Turið, and brings Turið and their daughter Tóra with him to the Faroe Islands. His relationship with Tróndur is rather unfriendly but peaceful.

When Ólavur Tryggvason came to power in Norway, he sent Sigmundur to the Faroes, and he managed to Christianize the islands, even Tróndur was at last forced to accept the Christian faith. The relationship between Sigmundur and Tróndur develops from bad to worse, and Tróndur and his men attack Sigmundur. Sigmundur escapes, and he, his fosterbrother Tórir and a third man try to swim from Skúvoy to Suðuroy. Sigmundur comes alive ashore in Sandvík, but is murdered by the local farmer Tórgrímur Illi, who hides his body. Tróndur now becomes chief over all of the islands.

Tróndur had taken Leivur - son of Øssur (son of Havgrímur) who was killed by Sigmundur - as his fosterson. He proposes to Tóra on Leivur's behalf, and she agrees to marry Leivur on the condition that he can swear that he had not killed her father; he has to promise to find out what has happened to Sigmundur as well. Tróndur, who has probably known the truth, now goes to Suðuroy and conjures forth the dead Sigmundur, and the farmer on Suðuroy is hanged. Leivur and Tóra marry, they get a son, young Sigmundur, who becomes the fosterson of Tróndur.

Sigurður, the man who had killed Sigmundur's son in Norway, makes Turið an offer of marriage on behalf of his brother. Turið is surprisingly forthcoming, and asks

him to come back for a final answer. Tóra and Leivur now hurry to Tróndur's farm to rescue their son, who would become a hostage if they killed one of Tróndur's men. When Sigurður returns, both he and his brother are killed by Leivur, and Tróndur dies out of anger.

## Sandoy

Here the grass grows from the shores to the hilltops and with its 13 býlingar - settlements mentioned in the oldest preserved land register from 1584 - Sandur was one of the largest and wealthiest pre-industrial agricultural societies in the Faroes. Today around 1470 people live in the area. Sandoy is rich with history and stories, through the centuries the people here have preserved old customs, and they are accomplished storytellers.

According to the Færeyinga Saga a man lived there in the Viking age named Snæúlvur. Local legend tells, that he lived at Krossi by the church (i.e. við Kirkjugarð) and that he had fled from the Hebrides because of a charge of manslaughter. Snæúlvur was Havgrímur í Hovi's father-in-law, but did not support him in his attack on Brestir and Beinir.

## Við Kirkjugarð heima á Sandi

Við Kirkjugarð heima á Sandi The site of Við Kirkjugarð (i.e. 'by the churchyard') in the village of Sandur has quite a special position in the archaeology of the Faroe Islands. As Sandur is one of the largest and wealthiest

*The site of Við Kirkjugarð in the village of Sandur has quite a special position in the archaleology of the Faroe Islands.*
                                                        *Photo: S. V. Arge*

agricultural societies, there can be no doubt, that ever since the first settlers, who were farmers, arrived at the islands in the Viking Period - the landnám period - this village must have been among the most prominent in the rural societies of that time.

## The church

Archaeological excavations have been carried out spasmodically in and outside the church in Sandur. These investigations have revealed traces of settlement activity within the whole churchyard area south of the church dating to the Viking Period.

When the first archaeological excavation in Sandur took place in 1969-70, efforts were focused within the actual church. The results

were outstanding and rather unexpected, as what was found were the remains of five successive churches under the present one, built in 1839. The oldest church was a small single-aisled stave church, as we know them from Norway, and dated to the 11th century. Thus, all in all six churches have been built one on the top of the other on this very spot.

## Viking activity and burials

In 1989 11 graves were uncovered in the extended area of the churchyard to the south of the church, of which 7 were excavated. The burials extend northwards beneath the old churchyard. The site gives the impression of a well-regulated cemetery consisting of a series of burials placed end to end in a number of more or less parallel rows; so none of the graves overlap. All of the graves are aligned east-west and all of the uncovered skeletons lay with their skulls pointing west.

The objects recovered from the graves can be classified as personal belongings more than regular gifts, e.g. finger rings, pearls of bone, glass and amber and iron knives. One of the buried, a young man, had been buried with an iron knife which had thin silver threads entwined around the handle, and he had a bronze finger ring; he also had a pouch or a purse - possibly a woven pouch - containing a leather purse. In this pouch were seven plain lead weights - three pairs, each pair contained a circular and a rectangular weight. Also a strap end was found in the grave, ornamented with an animal head and with a piece of leather still riveted to the opposite end; further a bronze fragment was found, which was decorated with an interlaced motif of Irish origin, and some small silver fragments.

*The brooch from Sandur. Cast bronze brooch with Scandinavian Viking decoration from the 10th century.*
*Photo: Per á Hædd*

In one of the graves a clipped Cufic Arab coin was found, - the first and only coin of this type found in the islands so far. This has been identified as a late 9th century imitation of an Abbasid-style dirhem, which may be suggestive for dating the burial to the mid 10th century.

It is interesting to mention, that the only Viking coin hoard found in the Faroes so far was found in this churchyard by a grave digger in 1863. The hoard consisted of 98 silver coins dating from the period of around AD 1000-1080/90. The coins came from what we now know as Germany, England, Ireland, Hungary, Norway and Denmark. For reasons we only can guess, the owner wished to conceal the coins and buried them sometime around AD 1090. Similarly, for one reason or another, the coins were never recovered and lay undisturbed until 1863.

We must suppose, that around AD 1000, at the time when it was commonly presupposed that the Faroes were conforming to Christianity, there existed a settlement here, important enough to warrant the erection of a church. The settlement activity on the site continued for a period after which the site was abandoned. Only the church and the churchyard remained up to recent times.

## Phosphate-survey

In the fields northwest of the church site, which have been cultivated for centuries, a survey showed especially high phosphate values, which could indicate a settlement area. But there were no signs of any

*Norwegian coin from the Viking coin hoard discovered in the Sandur churchyard in 1863.*
Photo: The National Museum of the Faroe Islands

settlement at the site at all. The explanation of these high phosphate values was at last revealed in the summer of 2000, when large parts of the cliffs eroded. Deep cultural layers were then exposed in the cliffs, situated just off and below the fields which were phosphate-surveyed. The phosphate values from the field and the cultural layers visible in the eroded cliffs derive from an extensive settlement in that area - a settlement to which we hitherto had no knowledge.

## Undir Junkarinsfløtti

The cliffs at this site, further 80 meters to the north of the church, were heavily eroded and stone structures in several phases as well as regular cultural layers became visible. A trench was made into the cliff to investigate the character of these cultural layers.

The layers were up to 2 meters thick and from the deepest layer up to the turf was 3.4 meters. The thickness of the single layers

varied. They mostly consisted of sand and sandy layers containing variable amounts of humus. Also characteristic were deposits of charcoal and ashes with a variety of heat-cracked stones from the beach. The latter are very characteristic for settlement layers deriving from the Viking and Medieval period in the Faroe Islands. Another characteristic feature was the huge amounts of very well preserved animal bones of all kinds - from oxen, sheep, pigs, fish and especially from birds. More regular findings were fragments from soapstone vessels, a spindle whorl also of soapstone, and fragments of local pottery as well. Perhaps the most interesting object was a brooch of bronze, which was found almost at the bottom of the layers. The closest parallel of the type - a circular conical shape - are some brooches found in a few burials in Iceland, dating from the 10th century. The provenance of this type of brooches is meant to be eastern Scandinavia or Saami from Northern Norway.

The cultural layers were exposed at a distance of 80-90 m north to another locality called Undir Breytasandi. After the removal of sand and other debris, it was evident the structures visible here were the remains of a 2 to 2.3 meters broad ruin constructed at right angles into the slope, into which it was only possible to excavate to a depth of 4.2 meters from the slope edge. The double walls are approx. 1.5 meters thick, well made and constructed from stone. Based on the few artefacts, mainly iron nails and lumps of rust, the shape of the building and the way the building has been set into the landscape it may be interpreted as a boathouse - but then the coastline must have changed since then.

The coast and the shoreline by the bay of Sandur have altered considerably within recent times, so we have to imagine that the topographical conditions - the coast and the cliffs - have been submitted to considerable changes during the centuries.

Ongoing research and restricted archaeological excavations in this area to the north of the old church site in the years 2003 and 2004 have revealed astonishing results. For the first time in the Faroes it has been possible to deal with an extraordinary wellpreserved collection of animal bones which are of the greatest interest in describing the sites' economy and peoples' exploitation of the natural resources. The investigations in Junkarinsfløttur tell us about early farming strategy, e.g. pig farming, practised on the Faroes during the Viking period and the early Middle Ages, just as in Iceland and Greenland, but which we up to

now have had practically no prior knowledge of, as this practice was abandoned sometime during the Middle Ages. Characteristic for the site is also the large collection of bird bones proving that fowling has played a surprisingly major part in the Viking economy when compared to cattle and sheep breeding.

In a cultural and archaeological context, the church site at Sandur and its surroundings must be recognised as a very remarkable one. The archaeological record from the site leaves us with the impression of a high status Faroese society with strong links to the outside world. Recent 14-carbon dating has dated the oldest activity here at the early Viking Period - a period which had been largely unknown in Faroese archaeology to date. As such, the site provides material for a re-evaluation of our view of the prehistoric settlement on this location and of the early history of the islands as a whole. The areas by the church site of Sandur both historically and archaeologically constitute some of the most interesting and promising research possibilities in the Faroe Islands.

## Húsavík

In Húsavík there are 3  býling-settlements, mentioned in the 1584 land register: Heimi á Garði, Suðuri á Bø and Suður í Haga (now deserted). Local tradition and settlement remains evidence further habitation in the village, e.g. í Kvíggjagili. Characteristic of the village is that all the infields (cultivated fields) are located on the southern side of the river, Stórá.

*Húsavík on Sandoy.*                                                    Photo: S. V. Arge

## The Dame of Húsavík

At Heimi á Garði the remains of the
farmhouses are still visible that húsfrúgvin í
Húsavík (the Dame of Húsavík), Guðrun
Sjúrðardóttir from Norway once owned. The
buildings are said to have been placed round
a paved courtyard. The remains of the main
house on the southern side of the courtyard
are the most visible today. Upon this stone
foundation the Stokkastova (log house) was
standing until about 2-300 years ago.

Guðrun Sjúrðardóttir owned great land in
Húsavík and Sandoy. Some letters, written in
about the period 1403-1405 tell us, that she
was from Bergen in Norway, and daughter of
Sjúrður Hjalt in Finnegården and owned
land in Norway and in the Shetlands too.

The legend tells that the log house which
she built for herself in Húsavík was drifted
from Norway, cut up so that it could be
erected at once. Part of the stone wall which
she had built round the churchyard still
stands; the walls of her hay-barn, the
foundations of her boathouse, and the paved
courtyard between the village houses, remain
also as memorials of the Dame of Húsavík.

There are many local stories about her
most of which describe her as an evil, harsh,
stern and hot-tempered woman, but
intelligent as well.

It is said that she buried alive two of her
women-servants, one in Teigur, the other,
who was called Brynhild, in Brynhild´s
Howe. All the large stones that are to be seen

here, she got the water-kelpie (njuggle) from lake Lítlavatn to drag down to her home from the mountains.

In the village of Skarvanes she had land brought into cultivation. She rune bound the infield, so that no stone from the cliffs would fall down on to it, though there was no fence around it.

## The church

The church is from the year of 1863 and built from stone. The altar piece was painted by the famous Danish artist Sven Havsteen-Mikkelsen.

## Jógvansbreyt

Jógvansbreyt is a fisherman's house, built in 1870 as a typical Faroese dwelling house from that period. The house is listed and is owned by Føroya Forngripafelag (The Faroese Museum Society).

## Skúvoy

The island Skúvoy is not large, only 56 people live on the island today, but it is rich in cultural and natural history. The largest birdcliffs in the Faroe Islands are to be found here and it is not far to go fishing at fishing banks. The westside of the island is like a castle standing up from the ocean, and the island may well have been a preferred chief's residence in the Viking age. The brothers Brestir and Beinir had a farm on Skúvoy and they reigned over half of the Faroe Islands. It was here that, Sigmundur Brestisson, according to the Færeyinga Saga, erected the first Christian church in the Faroes after returning back from Ólavur Tryggvason in Norway.

According to a legend after the Black Death had raged on Skúvoy (ca 1350), there was only one woman left in the village. Her name was Sunnuva. But on the north side of the island, Norði á Dal, Rannvá dwelled. She was the farmer's daughter and was entitled to

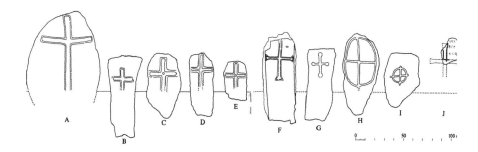

*The Skúvoy stones from the old churchyard at Ólansgarður in Skúvoy. The largest is the so-called Sigmundarsteinur.*

*Illustration: K. J. Krogh*

*Sigmundarsteinur in Ólansgarður in Skúvoy.*
*Photo: Rögnvaldur Guðmundsson*

inherit the farm, but her foster mother wanted her own daughter to inherit the farm and made Rannvá stay Norði á Dal looking after the oxen. She stayed there along with two illegitimate children, while the plague was raging in the village. She avoided the plague, and her son became tenant of the farm, and his four sons took over after him.

## Ólansgarður

In 1909 - 10 and again in 1921-22 the islanders started making a new cemetery on the same spot where the legend told that the old cemetery had been - at Ólansgarður, some hundred meters south of the modern village of Skúvoy. According to the legend it was here at his farm in Ólansgarður that

Sigmundur Brestisson had the first church built and a cemetery too, but that people stopped using it after the Black Death. They were afraid of being infected and made a new church yard in the village.

In the eastern half of the church yard they found coffins turning NW-SE. In the western half of the cemetery were found some stones with incised crosses on them. The only stone that by that time stood upwards was the so-called Sigmundarsteinur.

They found nine whole stones and two in pieces. All were made from basaltic rocks, except for one which was made from reddish tuff. One stone had two crosses carved into it, one on each side. The crosses are made in different styles: Wheel crosses, both a wheel and a cross have been carved into the stone, and latin crosses incised into the stone.

Different opinions are held on the origins and the date of the cross slabs. Some considered that they resemble stones, that have been found in Ireland and in the Scottish celtic area, and the stones therefore must be from the times prior to the Norse settlement at around the year of 800AD. Others have doubted this hypothesis, dating the stones according to the style of the crosses, and they believe that the stones - even though they seem Irish - are still more likely to come from the Norse period and after the propagation of Christianity in the Faroe Islands. According to recent research the closest parallels are to be found in the Hebrides in Scotland.

*The traditional Faroese dance is a chain-dance from the Medieval Periode. Some of the ballads have their motives from the Færeyinga Saga.*
Photo: Rögnvaldur Guðmundsson

One fragment of a runic stone that was found on Skúvoy in 1982 is a piece of yet an other cross stone. Runologically the stone can be dated to the period of 1000/1050 - 1150. The piece of stone was found on the bedrock below the village, where it has probably been thrown out with ashes from the steep slope. It is most likely that it originally came from Ólansgarður and it may be indicative for dating the cross stones from there.

The cemetery at Ólansgarður hasn't always been on its own. While making roads by Ólansgarður in the 1960s ancient settlement remains were found and during investigations done in 1989 to the east of Ólansgarður, observations were made of cultural layers which could indicate a settlement there. According to myth the old landing place was below Ólansgarður, because of the level beach and the low slope. These circumstances have likely changed through times, since we know how coastlines have changed at other places in the country, and today the landing place is further north.

All these indications seem to prove that a place of residence has been at Ólansgarður since at least Viking times. If one is to believe the Færeyinga Saga, Brestir and Beinir lived here - and perhaps even Sigmundur Brestisson!

## Further information
*www.natmus.fo*
*www.tourist.fo*

*Here is a gift I give you Tore Hund, which I expect you will use. Here is the spear which went through Asbjørn my son, and there is still blood upon it. You should throw this spear from your hand so that it will stand in King Olaf's breast; and this I can tell you, that you will be named coward in every man's mouth, if you don't avenge Asbjørn.*

(From Heimskringla)

## The story about Asbjørn Selsbane of Trondenes

In the saga about Olav the Holy from Heimskringla or "The Chronicle of the Kings of Norway", by Snorre Sturlason, one of the most important and powerful noble families in Hålogaland, the Bjarkøy and Trondenes family is mentioned:

*"There was a man named Sigurd Thoreson, a brother of Tore Hund of Bjarkey Island. Sigurd was married to Sigrid Skjalg's daughter, a sister of Erling. Their son, called Asbjørn, became as he grew up a very able man. Sigurd dwelt at Thrandarnes, and was a very rich and respected man. He had not gone into the king's service; and Tore in so far had attained higher dignity than his brother, that he was the king's*

*The medieval church at Trondenes. To the left Trondenes Historical Centre.*
Photo: Trondarnes Distriktsmuseum

*Asbjørn on his way to revenge Tore Sel
with a sword hidden under the robe.*
Photo: Trondarnes Distriktsmuseum

*lenderman. But at home, on his farm, Sigurd
stood in no respect behind his brother in
splendour and magnificence."*

Asbjørn of Trondenes was only 18 when
his father Sigurd died and a great
responsibility was laid on his shoulders. The
reputation and authority of the chieftain was
linked to wealth and the worship of the gods.
The sacrifices to the Norse gods which took
place in autumn, winter and spring were
important and mead brewed from honey and
barley was drunk at these feasts called *"blot"*.
Though they had converted to Christianity
they still had three *"blots"* every year.

Asbjørn had to travel south to buy grain
after several crops failures. He had relatives
on his mother's side in the south which he
hoped would help him, even though King
Olav had forbidden people to sell grain to
North-Norwegians by law. Snorre tells that
when Asbjørn first left in 1022 A.D. to buy
corn he *"launched a trading vessel ... which
was built like an ocean-going ship"* with a 20
man crew.

On his way south he stopped at Karmøy
where the kings man Tore Sel was in charge

and, when he was asked, Asbjørn told Tore
about his mission. Tore strongly disagreed
with what Asbjørn was about to do, but
upon leaving Asbjørn accepted Tore's

*"Tore Hund" holding the spear "Selshemnaren".*
Photo: Trondarnes Distriktsmuseum

*A picture from the exhibition illustrating Tore Hund attacking King Olav and killing him.*
Photo: Trondarnes Distriktsmuseum

invitation to visit him on his way back. Asbjørn visited his powerful uncle Erling and was able to buy grain from his slaves. When Asbjørn later returned to Karmøy he was robbed and humiliated by Tore Sel who not only took his corn and malt, but also stole his brand new sail. Asbjørn was deeply offended, he suffered a lot from gossip and mockery the following year and was not able to carry out his social duties as a chieftain.

Asbjørn, who was a very proud man, suffered because of these events and before long he desided to have his revenge on his tormentor. When he sailed to take revenge the following year,  Snorre says:

*"Asbjørn had a long-ship standing in the noust (shipshed), and it was a snekke (cutter) of*

*twenty benches; and after Candlemas (February 2, 1023), he had the vessel put in the water, brought out all his furniture, and rigged her out.  He then summoned to him his friends and people, so that he had nearly ninety men all well armed."*

He sailed south and arrived at the outer coast of Karmt Island. Dressed as a poor man he walked across the island and sneaked into the hall where the King was the guest of honour. Tore Sel stood before the high seat and bragged to the king how he had humiliated the young chieftain from Trondenes.  This became too much for Asbjørn who drew his sword and :

*"The stroke took him (Tore Sel) in the neck, so that the head fell upon the table before the king, and the body at his feet, and the table-cloth was*

*Trondenes Historical Centre*                                      *Photo: Frank S. Andreassen. Nettfoto*

*soiled with blood from top to bottom. The king ordered him to be seized and taken out."*

Luckily Asbjørn had several powerful allies, included his relatives from his mother`s side, who helped to save his life by making an agreement with the king. Asbjørn got King Olav`s permission to visit his farm at Trondenes before carrying out the arrangement. When Asbjørn came home he discussed the situation with his uncle Tore Hund. They both decided that the agreement should be brokened and as a result of this Asbjørn was outlawed. All of the King`s followers became aware of this, and the following year 1024 A.D., Asbjørn was killed with a spear on his way home from the Vågan gathering in Lofoten.

After his burial, Sigrid (his mother) gave the spear to Tore Hund in Altevågen at Trondenes, and with her words to this very powerful man, she not only showed her own personal power, but also demonstrated how powerful women were in the viking age:

*"Here is a gift I give thee, which I expect thou wilt use. Here is the spear which went through Asbjørn my son, and there is still blood upon it, to remind thee that it fits the wound thou hast seen on the corpse of thy brother's son Asbjørn. It would be a manly deed, if thou shouldst throw this spear from thy hand so that it stood in Olaf's breast; and this I can tell thee, that thou wilt be named coward in every man's mouth, if thou dost not avenge Asbjørn."*

The spear was called Selshemnaren (Sels`s avenger).

The revenge was fulfilled in 1030 at the Battle of Stiklestad when Tore Hund slew the king. After being murdered King Olav was canonized and named St. Olav, and the whole country was now baptised in the Christian faith.

This story is truly one of the most significant events in Norwegian prehistory. By the death of King Olav the old family traditions and Viking period ended. The country was under the rule of one Christian king and the Middle Ages began. Christianity became widespread and the Norse gods were abandoned.

## Trondenes Historical Centre and nearby surroundings
### The exhibition
The story of Asbjørn Selsbane is displayed in our exhibition. With several tableaux, archaeological artefacts and multivision, the dramatic events are played out to allow the visitor to experience the prehistory of Trondarnes.

### Sites of boathouses at Altevågen
Altevågen is on the west side of Trondenes and is an interesting area containing two boathouse sites and five gravemounds. From the saga text we know that Asbjørn, on his journeys, used a knarr, a Norse trading vessel which was approximately 15 m long and had a crew of 20 men. The saga text also mentions that the longship was launched when he set out to revenge himself on Tore Sel. The ship had 40 rowers and could carry 90 men.

The boathouse sites correspond in size to the saga`s description of events surrounding Asbjørn Selsbane Sigurdsson in 1022-1024 A.D. Local tradition has always connected "Stornaustet" (the large boathouse) and "Lillenaustet" (the small boathouse) with Asbjørn`s vessels. Snorre Sturlasson`s "The saga of Olav the Holy" is an important written source in this respect.

The results from the archaeological excavations in the area, give us enough evidence to say that the boathouses definitely were in use when Asbjørn was alive. The archaeological findings concure with the written sources. Snorre may have based his saga about Asbjørn "Selsbane" Sigurdsson on a lost document. The details in the saga and the correspondence with the ancient monuments in Altevågen suggest this may have been the case.

### The cultural path
The path starts at Trondenes Historical Centre and takes you to the church and then past the vicarage where Asbjørn`s farm was located. Further on the path takes you over to Altevågen where the boathouse tofts are located. Several sign boards are set up to inform visitors and a booklet is also avalable which gives information on other historical sites and also decribes the natural wildlife and biology in the near vicinity.

### The church at Trondenes
The church (1200-1400 A.D.) is located where the earlier hedonistic chieftain-seat lay for 1000 years before Christianity came. The rise of Christianity in the 11th century brought the most extensive cultural change in

*Excavation in the big boathouse where Asbjørn kept his longship.*     *Photo: Trondarnes Distriktsmuseum*

the history of Northern Norway. Trondenes was then incorporated into the Roman Catholic Church.

The vicarage next to the church is situated on a 9000 sq.m. farm mound and archaeologists have found the remains of buildings, rubbish tips and discarded items from settlements dating back 2500 years. It was in this area Asbjørn Selsbane`s farm was located.

## Other relevant sites
### Bjarkøy - The home of Tore Hund
In connection with a project called "Fotefar mot nord" there are several cultural paths with sign boards and booklets to guide people along some of the interesting prehistoric and historic sites of northern Norway. One such path has been made at Bjarkøy which, in the Viking period, had established itself as the seat of the mightiest family in North Norway; the Bjarkøy Clan. There are very many traces of Viking settlement and interaction on the island, all part of its prehistory, and a number of these have been chosen to represent this exciting period of the past.

### Viking Boathouse Tofts at Tjeldøya
In Nordland county on the island of Tjeldøya, at Sand, lies a boathouse toft from the Viking period. This very large boathouse is 38 m long and was built to contain a large ship.

*Modern Vikings outside the church at Trondenes.*                    *Photo: Trondarnes Distriktsmuseum*

In order to visit this boathouse you must travel south of Harstad on the road RV 83. When you pass the Tjeldsund bridge you will follow E 10 further south until you see a sign with the name Ramsund. There you should turn right and follow the road 824 which crosses the Ramsund bridge. Take a left and stop in Sand where you will find the boathouse. There is a sign board at the site with further information.

## Further information

*www.tdm.no*
*www.destinasjonharstad.no*

*Olav Tvennumbruni went from Lofotr to Iceland and settled the whole area of Skeid between Thjorsa and Sandlækur in South Iceland and lived at Olafsvellir. He was married to Áshild, and they had three sons [...].* (Fom the book of Settlement)

*One theory explaining Olav's travel is the fury of King Harald Fairhair. Several chieftains got into conflict with him and fled away. Shortage of land is another possible theory.*

# Lofotr - the Vikingmuseum at Borg, Lofoten, Norway

## The Saga

Lofoten in Northern Norway is mentioned in several Sagas; mainly the *Sagas of the Norwegian Kings* (Kringla Heimsins), *Icelandic Family Sagas* in addition to the *Landnåma* book, also referred to as the Book of Conquest. Several of the Sagas referring to Viking Age events were actually written down some hundred years later and the fact that the authors not were contemporary with the described events is a source-critical problem.

The North of Norway and the Hålogaland area is mentioned in several Sagas, and these, together with the Landnåma book, constitute the beginning of our journey. The Landnåma book is a register of early settlers at Iceland in the period 870-930 AD and the book as we know it was written down in the 12th century based upon family registers. There are three different preserved versions of the Landnama book; Sturlubook, Hauksbook and Melabok. All of them mention Olaf Tvennumbruni and here follows an extract of the text in Hauksbook.

*The 83 meter reconstructed longhouse at Borg.*

Photo: Rögnvaldur Guðmundsson

*Viking banquet in the Chieftains hall.*

*Photo: Rögnvaldur Guðmundsson*

*"Olav Tvennumbrune het en mann som fòr fra Lofot til Island. Han tok hele Skeid mellom Tjorså og Kvitå og Sandløk, og var en stor hamram. Olav bodde på Olavsvellir, og han er hauglagt i Brunahaugen ved Vardefjell. Olav var gift med Åshild, og sønnene deres var Helge trauste og Tore drive..... Den tredje sønnen til*

*Olav var Vade som var far til Gerd."* (Hauksbook, page 377)

The quote tells about Olaf Tvennumbruni, who settled down at Olafsvellir in the south of Iceland together with his family: the wife Åshild and the sons

*The Landnåmabook (the Hauksbook version) where Olav Tvennumbruni is mentioned on page 377.*
*Photo: Lofotr- the Vikingmuseum at Borg*

*The reconstruction and the original dwelling.*
Photo: Lofotr- the Vikingmuseum at Borg

Helge, Tore and Vade. According to the story, Olaf was a chieftain from the island of "Lofot", and historians agree that Lofot can be interpreted and identified as the medieval name of Vestvågøy, the name probably originating from a certain area of this island. "Lofot" *might* be interpreted in terms of topographical conditions in the Borg-area.

Why did Olaf leave for Iceland? During this period there was tremendous settlement expansion and many Norwegians left for Iceland between 870-930, with their families, retainers, slaves and animals. Maybe some left their country because of political disagreements while others were driven by a desire for new land. There was also the great attraction of power and glory in the new lands to conquer in the North Atlantic.

Archaeological distribution indicates at least three chieftains' residences in Lofoten: Buksnes and Borg on the island of Vestvågøy and Hov on the island of Gimsøy. In contrast to the archaeological material, the written sources referring to such power structures are rather poor.

The Viking-museum is a site-museum, represented by a reconstruction of a chieftain's long-house. The area was farmland until 1981 when a local farmer ploughed deeper than usual on the Borg-height. The soil turned out to be unusually dark and in the furrows pieces of glass and potsherds showed up. The artefacts were classified as

*The museum has two reconstructed boats from the Gokstad find. The Viking ship Lofotr in the background and the little femkeiping in the front.*
Photo: Kjersti Jacobsen

French and German glasses and pottery, 1200-1300 years old and found this far north for the first time. Surveys and excavations were begun and the results brought a whole new perspective to the relationship between Lofoten, Southern Scandinavia and the rest of Europe.

Archaeological excavations revealed the remains of a longhouse, 83 m in length. An inter-Scandinavian research project converged on the site from 1983-1989, and scholars established the fact that this was the largest building ever found anywhere in the Viking world. The building commanded a wide view, making the area easy to control, and the house must have been visible a long way off. The Borg area was probably a sacred site, from the heathen period at least and up to the church of the present day.

There were two main phases of longhouse building: the first was a 67-metre long building erected in the 6th c. and during the 8th c. this building was extended so that at the beginning of the Viking Age the house

*The Eltoft sword-hilt.*
Photo: Are Pedersen

measured 83 metres. The house was divided into five main rooms, including a living quarter, lobby, a hall, store and byre. After the excavation, the foundation walls were marked on the original site, as well as the posts, and a modern reconstruction was built close by. The reconstruction is based on the excavations and the structures discovered including the floor plan, the division of the rooms and the situation of the hearths and walls. The height of 9 metres and the roof construction are qualified guesses, calculated on the basis of recent research upon Nordic Viking houses.

*The 40 meter long boat-house from Holsneset in the Buksnesfjord.*
Photo: Lofotr- the Vikingmuseum at Borg

*A cairn and a standing stone from the burial field at Holsøya.*     Photo: Lofotr- the Vikingmuseum at Borg

In the immediate area you can find collapsed walls from long-ship boathouses, several settlement sites, burial mounds and a so-called courtyard-site. All together, this is evidence of an Iron Age power centre.

*Access:* The museum is open for groups all year, and for individuals daily from mid May to mid September.

### Other relevant sites

There are attractions throughout Lofoten; traditional fishing villages, galleries, craftworkers, farms, museums, bird-sanctuaries, beaches, mountains to climb and much much more.

Saga-related sites are mainly situated on Vestvågøy, Austvågøy and Gimsøy. On Gimsøy you can experience huge longship

boathouses, house dwellings and a court site as well as a standing stone and grave mounds.

Close to Borg a courtyard-site is identifiable. The remains of four and a half houses are vaguely visible on the surface, and in addition, several structures on the surface could be interpreted as possible house-structures. The complex is situated 75 m from the shore. Some hundred metres from the site, two boat-houses have been recorded. The courtyard-site and the boathouses are situated on private property and are inaccessible.

### Eltoft

A well preserved burial-mound is situated at Eltoft. The mound is 18 m in diameter and 2 m height. In the 1930s, during ploughing, a local farmer discovered a sword in his field. The farmer probably ploughed through a grave and the sword is today exhibited at the Vikingmuseum at Borg. The owner of this sword must have been a powerful person; the grip consists of 6 bronze-plates, connected with nails, decorated with silver and was probably made during the 9th century. The large burial-mound and various artefacts indicate that this area was important in the context of its political, economic and social status in Iron Age society.

## Buksnesfjorden

The Buksnesfjord area has a large number of structures from the Iron Age, and the area is considered to have been important during the early Iron-Age.

At Holsneset you can see the largest boat-house in Northern Norway. The structure is oriented North-South, situated just beside a smaller bay on the south-side of Holsøya. The fjord has several locations suitable for landing boats as it is sheltered behind low-lying mountains. This area was probably also the base of a chieftain. The size of the boat-house is amazing being a full 40 metres and it could have stored a "30-sesse", rowed by 60 men, one of the largest boats of Norway's medieval fleet.

*Access:* A pathway leads to the boat-house.

## Holsøya

A large burial field is situated on Holsøya. The island became the property of the

*The Lofot-cathedral and the "Trollstein" between Kabelvåg and Svolvær.*
Photo: Lofotr- the Vikingmuseum at Borg

University of Tromsø in 1969, and contains around sixty burial mounds scattered among six separate fields.

*Access:* The island is property of the University of Tromsø and is open to the public though occasionally high tide will make the island inaccessible.

## Einangen

This very large burial-cairn is one of the most spectacular sites on Vestvågøy. Over the last few centuries its size has diminished, due to re-use of the construction material in stone walls in the area. The present cairn is a restoration, made after its excavation. The cairn was probably constructed during a time equivalent to the Roman period.

*Access:* The cairn is accessible from the main road. From the parking place at the top of the pass you can enjoy a panoramic view and also see the cairn.

Furthermost out in Lofoten you can see the "Norwegian fishing village museum" and learn more about life in the fishing village and the Lofoten fishery over the past 200 years.

## Vågan

On the island of Austvågøy, close to the village of Kabelvåg, you can visit the site of the medieval town Vågar. Excavations have been carried out here since the 1970s, and some artefacts are exhibited at the "Lofotmuseet", in conjunction with the history of the Lofoten fisheries. The main theme is fishing in Lofoten, the development

of stockfish exports in the medieval ages as well as the first town in North-Norway, Vågar. You can visit the site of the old medieval town nearby, as well as traces of a Saami settlement. The "Trollstein" and the Lofot-cathedral are also well worth a visit.

This structure with its cross is obviously of a religious nature. The stone is about 1x2x1 metres, and one of the vertical sides has a cross carved in it about 75 cm in height. The shape of the cross is similar to those used around the year 1000 AD in the north of Norway.

Such monuments are not a common feature, the closest parallels outside of Norway are to be found at the Faroe Islands and the Orkney Islands.

The site is easily accessible.

## Further reading

Munch, Gerd Stamsø, Johansen, Olav Sverre and Roesdal, Else. 2003. *Borg in Lofoten. A chieftain's farm in North Norway.*
Berge, Geir. 2004. *Lofoten, a travellers guide.*

## Further information

*www.lofotr.no*
*www.museums-of-lofoten.no*
*www.lofotmuseet.no*
*www.lofoten-info.no*

*King Harald Fairhair was the Viking king who defeated several petty kings in the Battle of Hafrsfjord and unified Norway into one kingdom sometimes between 868 and 900 AD. Harald Fairhair made Avaldsnes his home. He settled down here, died here, and he was buried close to the strait Karmsundet.*

# Avaldsnes, Norway's oldest throne, Karmøy, Norway

On the south-west coast of Norway you find the island Karmøy, known for its many archaeological finds and ancient monuments, and for its rich and exciting history.

The name Karmøy originates from the Old Norse word "Kormt" which means shelter. This long and narrow island protects the mainland from the North Sea and forms the strait "Karmsund". The ocean outside Karmøy is filled with underwater currents and skerries. Thus the ships were forced into the narrow Karmsund, which was the starting point of the protected ship lane called "The North Way" - Norway.

Strategically situated by this strait you find the ancient royal residence Avaldsnes which means "the ness of Ogvald."   The ancient skaldic poem Grimnismál tells that Thor, the god of thunder, wades the strait Karmsund every morning on his way to Yggdrasil, the tree of life.

*Photo: Archaeolocical museum, Stavanger*

*Kormt and Ormt*
*and two large rivers;*
*these shall Thor wade*
*every day when*
*he walks to deem*
*at the Yggdrasil Ash;*
*Thus the bridge of heaven*
*can burn;*
*warm is holy water*

## Where the myths and legends become tangible history

At Avaldsnes the heroic kings we know from the Islandic Sagas and skaldic poems become real, with their ships, gold rings and horses. Rich archaeological discoveries together with written sources make Avaldsnes a very important place when it comes to studying the history of the Vikings.

In the Viking Age, Avaldsnes stands out as a kingly centre of great strategic and political importance. It is no coincidence that some of the largest and most spectacular grave mounds in Norway, two of them ship burials, are found here. New research has dated these two ship burials to respectively the 8th and the 10th century.

*On the north side of the St. Olav's Church stands the Virgin Mary's Sewing Needle. Measuring 7.2 metres it is one of Norway's tallest standing stones, but originally it was taller. Local legends tell us that doomsday will come when the stone touches the church wall, so in times gone by the priests, under cover of darkness, have climbed up the stone and chipped pieces from the top, thus saving the world from destruction.*
*Photo: Ø. Iversen*

*Replica of a Viking ship at Avaldsnes.*
Photo: J. A. Hveding

At the same time, through new interpretations, the spotlight has been thrown on the old heroic sagas. These almost forgotten Icelandic sagas tell the story of named Avaldsnes kings in strong political environments as early as in the last part of the 7th century.

**Ship burials and named kings from the world of myths**

It 1998 the ship burial called Storhaug was dated back to the 8th century. In this burial mound a king had been buried in a large Scandinavian ship, surrounded by rich gifts that reflected close contact with the Carolingians. It has been suggested that the heroic king Halv might be the person that was buried in this ship.

The ship in the burial mound called Grønhaug was dated back to the first part of the 10th century, the same time as when the

*Figures of Harald Fairhair and Queen Gyda in Nordvegen History Centre.*          Photo: Ø. Iversen

dynasty founder Harald Fairhair died at Avaldsnes. This is the kind of grave one might expect that a Viking king of his status would get, and perhaps the ship burial Grønhaug is Harald Fairhair's burial place.

## Harald Farihair makes Avaldsnes Norway's oldest throne

King Harald Fairhair was the Viking king who defeated several petty kings in the Battle of Hafrsfjord and unified Norway into one kingdom sometimes between 868 and 900 AD. After the unification, he chose Avaldsnes as his most important kingly manor. According to the sagas, all of Harald's estates were in Rogaland and Hordaland.

Harald Fairhair made Avaldsnes his home. He settled down here, died here, and he was buried close to the strait Karmsundet.

## Eric Bloodaxe and Håkon The Good

Eric Bloodaxe was a victorious warrior, but violent of disposition, and unpopular in certain districts of Norway. The Norwegians sent a message to his youngest brother Håkon who returned to Norway equipped by his foster father, the English king Athalstan. Eric Bloodaxe fled from Norway to England where he became the last Scandinavian king of York.

In 953 Håkon had to fight a fierce battle at Avaldsnes against the sons of his brother Eric Bloodaxe. The battle is said to have been at the Bloodheights (Blodheia) that got its name from this event. Snorri Sturlason tells us that Håkon won the battle and that Eric's

*Håkon in battle against the sons of Eric Bloodaxe.*
*Ill. E. Werenskiold. Saga of Håkon the Good.*

son Guttorm died. The chronicler Agrip states that three of Eric's sons died in this battle.

> *Battle-slain, men above, the*
> *breaker-of-armrings let then*
> *sword-blades sing in strident*
> *song on the ness of Ogvald.*
> *There the Frey of flashing*
> *firebands-of-combat*
> *left for dead the doughty*
> *din-of shields' awakener*

## King Olav Tryggvason

Olav Tryggvason is said to have been the most handsome, greatest and strongest among men, and in sports no one could beat him. With a heavy hand Olav introduced Christianity in Norway. King Olav built the first church at Avaldsnes, and the Islandic Sagas describe that he several times was attacked by heathen forces at his royal manor here.

### Odin visits king Olav at Avaldsnes

The Islandic Sagas tell that the Viking god Odin came to Avaldsnes in disguise and told

Olav Tryggvason the stories about the legendary king Ogvald who had given his name to Avaldsnes. The next morning Olav discovers that the old storyteller have tried to poison him. Thus Olav understands that the old one-eyed man was Odin himself. Olav then goes out and opens several burial mounds at Avaldsnes. In one burial mond he finds the bones of a man, in another the bones of a cow.

### King Olav has the sorcerers drowned at Skrattaskjær

At Easter 998 a fully loaded ship with sorcerers and wizards came to Avaldsnes. They wanted to cast spells over king Olav Tryggvason because he had brought Christianity to Norway. The sorcerers made a thick black mist, but the mist went back on the sorcerers and blinded them.

Olav Tryggvason captured and tied the sorcerers up to some rocks out in the Karmsund. When the tide came in, the sorcerers drowned. Since then the rocks have been called Sorcerers skerries.

*The sorcerers are drowned at Skrattaskjær*
*Ill. H. Egedius. Saga of Olav Tryggvason*

*St Olav walks through the lines of Erling's men.*
*Ill. E. Werenskiold. Saga of St. Olav.*

## Olav Haraldson (Saint Olav)

Before Olav Haraldson became king of Norway, he fought as a Viking in many countries, among these was England where he helped the English king Æthelred against the Danes.

The Islandic Sagas tells that the king's farm manager at Avaldsnes, Tore Sel, in 1022 confiscated a load of grain that a man called Asbjørn had transported from his uncle Erling Skjalgson at Sola. The year after Asbjørn came back and killed Tore before the eyes of king Olav. Olav therefore sentenced Asbjørn to death. However, before the death-sentence was executed, Erling Skjalgson came to Avaldsnes with 1500 men from Jæren, and the king had to reprieve Asbjørn. This event stirred up bad blood between the families and led to the death of Olav at Stiklestad.

## Avaldsnes and the Kings of the Herioc sagas

### King Ogvald and his female warriors

Avaldsnes (Ogvaldsnes) has got its name from the legendary king Augvald or Ogvald

*St. Olav's church stands today as the most distinct and important monument in Avaldsnes. It was built by King Håkon Håkonson around 1250 as part of the royal manor complex. Håkon Håkonson dedicated the church to St. Olav, and the church became an important stopping place for pilgrims going to Nidaros. In the early 1300s Håkon V Magnusson made St Olav's church one of only four royal collegiate churches in Norway. Today St. Olav's church at Avaldsnes is the only one left.*    Photo: P. Mercer

who is supposed to have lived around 600 AD. Ogvald is called "the descendant of gods and the forefather of kings". He could trace his ancestry back to the first giant Ymir, who was formed at the same time as the great cow 'Audhumla' when the world was created at the meeting of fire and ice. Perhaps this is why Augvald had a holy cow that he would make sacrifices to.

Ogvald was a belligerent fellow who went on Viking raids to foreign countries and won great riches and acclaim. By winning a number of battles at sea, he conquered the

rulers who lived around the strait of Karmsund. He then set up court at Avaldsnes – the place that came to be called the peninsular, or "ness", of Ogvald.

Ogvald had two daughters who were shield-maidens and who fought with him in battle.

Shield-maidens were female warriors who could "ride the wind over land and sea". Together with his daughters and his holy cow Ogvald was killed in a battle against another king from Karmøy called Ferking or

*Photo: Ø. Iversen*

*Some of the finds from the Flag Mound.*
*The burial mound called "Flag Mound" was*
*excavated as early as 1835 and found to be a*
*chieftain's grave from the Late Roman Period*
*(250 and 300 AD). He was buried with more*
*gold than has been found in any other grave from*
*the same period in Scandinavia. The grave also*
*contained a lot of weapons and imported objects*
*that witness about close contact with the Romans.*
*Photo: Bergen Museum*

Varin. The shield-maidens were buried at
Ferkingstad, but Ogvald and his cow were
brought home to Avaldsnes and buried in the
King's Mound and the Cow's mound
respectively.

### King Hjørleiv and King Halv

Augvald got a son called Jøsur who got a son
called Hjør who got a son called Hjørleiv
«lover of women». According to skaldic
poems and heroic sagas, all of them were
kings of Rogaland and Hordaland.

One of Hjørleiv's sons was called Halv.
Twelve years old king Halv gathered the 60
best warriors from 11 counties, and these
men sailed as Vikings for 18 years. They were
legendary sailors who never found it

necessary to seek harbour when a storm blew
up, and on shore they fought close to their
enemies with short swords. But never did
Halv and his warriors attack women and
children, and it was prohibited for them to
touch any woman in a discourteous manner.
King Halv died around 750 AD.

*Halv*
*I saw him*
*swing his sword*
*with two hands.*
*With no shiled the proud prince faught*
*A more handsome*
*high-born*
*valiant warrior*
*of ornamented soul*
*will never be found again*
*(Saga of King Halv)*

### Further information
*www.nordvegen.info*
*www.vikinggarden.no*

*Test excavations at the King's mound.*
*Avaldsnes is still an archaeological treasury and the area is subject to strict preservation regulations. In August 2005 the Archaeological Museum in Stavanger made some test excavations at a height called the King's mound. Five new burial sites were found. None of the graves have yet been opened. Traces of settlement like post holes and fireplaces were also found. According to tradition this height was the place where the Viking kings had their Ting or Place of Justice. It is told that it was on this mound that Olav Tryggvason had the first local people baptised.*                                    Photo: Ø. Iversen

*Nordvegen History Centre.*
*In april 2005 Nordvegen History Centre, Avaldsnes was opened by queen Sonja. The centre tells the history of Avaldsnes from the Bronze Age to the Middle Ages when Avaldsnes was a national (at times also an international) centre of power. The focus is on Harald Fairhair who made Avaldsnes the first Royal Throne of Norway and on the other kings that we know from the Islandic Sagas.*                                    Photo: Ø. Iversen

*The Viking longhouse.*                                                                 Photo: Ø. Iversen

### *The Viking Farm Avaldsnes.*
*At Avaldsnes there is also a reconstructed Viking farm with a 25m long longhouse, a 32 m long boat house for a Viking warship and several smaller buildings.*

*The Viking boat house.*                                                                 Photo: Gunnar Colding

*At Gene fornby a "family" have been made up (a chieftain, his wife, children, maids, grandmother and so on) during the years. People who frequently work at Gene fornby have personified these personalities during the years, some of them totally identifying with their roll so hard that it is not possible to "change them" and get another person to have that specific roll.*

# Gene fornby - Iron Age farm, Örnsköldsvik, Sweden

## Gene fornby and the Saga-tradition

The archaeology of the area of Gene fornby in the northeastern part of Sweden belongs to the Roman Iron Age and the Migration Period between approximately 0 AD to 600 AD The farm at Gene fornby is the northernmost in the south Scandinavian longhouse style and reflects a cultural tradition reaching from Denmark and Germany up to Norway and Sweden. None of the more famous Viking sagas are directly connected with the area but despite this there is a wealth of local material existing in the area, still vivid in the minds of the community.

At Gene fornby many of these old, north Swedish sagas and stories are narrated as part of daily life and in meetings with visitors of all kinds, but few of them have a direct connection with particular sites. The story

*The longhouse of Gene fornby. Reconstruction of the second longhouse at Genesmon, dated approximately 300-600 AD.*

Photo: Agne Säterberg

about the grave in the village of Vågsnäs (Vågsnäsgraven) sometimes told at Gene fornby, is an exception and while this story is partly a "modern" one, it is narrated in the same way as all the other "real" sagas. The grave is located only 1 kilometre from the Gene farm and the oral story told goes as follows:

## The grave in Vågsnäs

*In 1978 a man, Helge Gidmark, in the village of Vågsnäs, called the museum in the town of Örnsköldsvik and asked them to come and look at an old grave outside his house. He was going to raise a garage where the grave was situated, and according to Swedish ancient law you must contact the authorities when you plan to build something that may cause damage to ancient remains. Helge told the archaeologists that he knew of the site as the "Russian grave" and he*

*was sure that it was a warrior from one of the Swedish-Russian wars that was buried there, complete with his weapons on his chest, on a skin from a bear. This was not unlikely and reflects the fact that Russians invaded the northern coast of Sweden in 1718.*

*The archaeologists at the museum first looked at their maps of ancient remains in the community and made a statement to the effect that " There was no grave or graveyard registered at the place the man told them about." At that time, the excavations of the Gene-farm had begun, and they just couldn't believe there were more ancient remains in the surroundings than those that had already been found. So they told Helge to take no notice of it and start to work. As work got underway, he became even surer that it was a grave mound, and once again he contacted the local museum. This time they came to look at the monument,*

*One of the mounds at the gravefield of Genesmon from the Roman Iron Age. These gravemounds are very similar to "the Russian grave" and they are all contemporary.*

Photo: Agne Säterberg

*Some of the family members by the open fire in the longhouse.*    Photo: Agne Säterberg

and after the first investigation they were also convinced that it was a quite damaged grave mound made up of stones and sand. *Together with volunteers from the villages in the surrounding area, the University of Umeå started an investigation of the grave. The "Russian grave" turned out to be much older than from 1718 and was actually dated as being from the Migration Period 400-600 AD, which made it contemporary with the graveyard at Genesmon only 1 kilometre away! The grave is a mound, typical for the Iron Age in Sweden, originally about 8 meters wide, and it contained bone material from a single person. Some grave gifts were found: a comb made of bone, some arrowheads, some bronze artefacts and 7 claws from a bear, which indicates that the person had been buried on a bear's skin. This custom is known from other places in Sweden, but is not commonly found.*

The interesting thing with this story is the fact that the oral tradition in the community was very strong, and the stories that have become the accepted "truth" will carry on being the "truth" for hundreds or even thousands of years: The person in the grave had weapons with him, and he was known as a warrior. The oral tradition, however, will change over time according to current society and what events are taking place in the vicinity. In time, it was difficult to explain why there was a grave amongst the houses in the small village. Graves should be in the graveyards by the churches, shouldn't they? Therefore the grave couldn't contain a normal Swedish person. It must have been a foreigner, most likely a Russian, since they had been plundering the coast several times, especially in 1718. By dating the grave however the additional aspects of the legend about the "Russian" were revealed as being untrue and it was established that this was instead an Iron Age man from about 500 AD, but on a skin from a bear with his weapons on his chest, just as Helge had said.

The grave in Vågsnäs is very similar to the 13 chieftain grave mounds close to the Gene farm, and since they burred their dead at home, the grave at Vågsnäs shows that there was a contemporary farm as close as 1 km from Genesmon.

*Hunting with bow and arrow- a daily work for the Iron Age farmer.* *Photo: Agne Säterberg*

## Genesmon and Gene fornby

In the mid 70s the community of Örnsköldsvik was going to build houses at Genesmon, a forested area close to the bay Bäckfjärden at the village of Gene. Since the archaeologists already knew of a graveyard at Genesmon with 13 grave mounds, they managed to get the area excavated, and very soon they found indications which pointed towards a large, prehistoric settlement. As a result no houses were built at Gene, but instead excavations by archaeologists from

*Listening to a good story.* *Photo: Agne Säterberg*

*Gathered around the table.*

*Photo: Agne Säterberg*

the university in Umeå began and lasted for 12 summers. The archaeologists found the remains of a large farm, probably a chieftain's farm, which existed from the year of 0 AD to 600 AD They found the remains of two large longhouses, each 40 meter long, an extraordinarily big smithy, a weaving-house, cultivation, a bronze casting foundry and much more. Many findings of iron, bronze and bone were made: tools, arrowheads, sickles, needles, fishhooks and a key, just to mention a few of them. Also 13 glass beads (probably imported) and a lot of burned clay and pottery were found. The people at Gene had been farmers who cultivated barley over an area of 3 acres, but had also lived by fishing and hunting.

The excavations were a sensation and a big step forward for the archaeology in the northern part of Sweden at that time. Before the 1970s no sedentary settlement from the Roman Iron age so far north in Sweden had been found, and the excavation at Genesmon revealed totally new facts about the Iron Age people in this area.

Even before the excavations were finished in 1989, the decision was made to reconstruct the farm again some 500 meters from the original site, and in accordance with the archaeological findings. A foundation was created which included the community of Örnsköldsvik, the university in Umeå, the county council and the county museum in Härnösand. Today the Mid Sweden Tourism board is also part of the foundation. In the beginning of the 90s the reconstruction of the big longhouse started, and after that a smithy, a barn for seed and a weaving pit were built. Gene fornby today shows the farm as we think it would have looked like in the 6th century AD Since the start Gene fornby has had three "legs" to build on: education, tourism and archaeological research. The farm is open for groups all year round to come on guided tours, Iron Age dinners, Iron Age activities, school-programs, conferences, markets and music-festivals. Iron Age dramas, "bygdespel", are also an important part of the annual activities, and in them the sagas play a considerable role. During the summer the farm is open for tourists every day and is presented as a living farm with an Iron Age family acting and doing Iron Age daily work. As a tourist you can also try Iron Age activities like baking bread and forging in the smithy.

## The longhouse of Gene fornby

The farm of Gene fornby has existed in two epochs: The first lasting from the year of 0 AD to 300 A.D, and the second lasting from 300 AD. to 600 AD These periods have had two, very similar longhouses, the northernmost ever found in Sweden representing the south-Scandinavian culture. A few kilometres north of Gene, in the parish of Arnäs, is the definitive border of the south Scandinavian culture in Sweden. Further north in Sweden no longhouses of this kind have been found and a different culture existed here during the Iron Age, with eastern influences.

The longhouse of Gene was reconstructed according to the findings of the excavation which included the marks of postholes in the ground, dark markings of the walls, finds of seeds and artefacts and the situation of the hearths etc. The house is 40 metres long, about 8 metres wide and divided into 6 different rooms. It was home for both the family of about 15 people and also their animals. There was housing for 8 cows, 20 sheep or goats and pigs, and a horse was stabled in the northern part of the house. The living room, "stugu", a storage room and threshing area were situated in the southern part. The walls were first made of clay mixed with manure from the cows, but after restoration in the years of 2003 and 2004 the wall material is now wood. On the southern part of the roof there is birch-bark and turf in several layers and on the northern part birch-bark and timber. The questions about which materials should be used in the outer wall and in the fillings in the inner one has never been solved, and what has been chosen has been as a result of qualified guesses. For the rest of the house, the excavations gave the answers. Thanks to the fact that the smithy caught fire we know a lot about the roofing, because the roof did not burn up. The turf on top of the roof put out the fire so the timber in the roof turned to coal and was therefore preserved and it was possible to see dimensions, techniques and type of material chosen. Also one of the longhouses had burnt down. The remains showed that the northern part of the house had a lighter roof, and the fact that the roof-supporting posts had burned deep into the postholes, pointed to a roof with no turf but with easily burnt materials on top. Since there are two ways to keep the birchbark in place, this part of the longhouse was given timber in the

*Scene from "Genespelet" in the summer of 2004.*                    *Photo: Gene fornby*

reconstruction to hold the birchbark. In the south part of the building the excavation showed that something had put out the fire, just like with the smithy and since the posts had larger dimensions, all pointed to turf on top of the roof. The longhouse of Gene fornby was a chieftain's house, extraordinarily big for this time in northern Sweden.

## The Sagalands project

The aim at Gene fornby has been to create a "living space", a place where visitors get a chance to experience their history with all

their senses and since the very beginning, in 1990, the objective has been to create an educational area suitable for tourists as well as for local schoolchildren. One way of doing this is storytelling, a natural human activity that keeps the history alive and binds together the culture of today with the culture of our ancestors 1500 years ago. The key phrase for all activities on the farm all year round is "Experience your past", and the Sagaland project at Gene fornby actually consists of those elements which make the farm come alive through the people involved namely storytelling, drama and music.

*Time to play after supper.*                                                   Photo: Agne Säterberg

As was said at the beginning, no famous Viking saga is connected with Gene and mostly only shorter stories are directly connected with the area. It is a fact that the farm existed some hundred years before people started to emigrate from Scandinavia to Iceland, Greenland and over the rest of the northern periphery area. At Gene fornby therefore many stories from the local region are told, most of them very old and related for example to nature or to "Vittra", the small people living alongside the human inhabitants. "Vittra" seem to be a common phenomenon in the whole saga world, but with many different names. The Vitter stories in northern Sweden, the area to which Gene belongs, often tell how the "Vittra"

either help the people of a farm or bring unhappiness over them because of bad treatment. There is often a strong moral to the stories telling how best to deal well or badly with the "Vittra".

The other parts of the saga tradition are Sagas interpreted through dramatic performances, roll playing and above all the Geneplay, "Genespelet". Beginning in the year of 2001, a group of people started to create an annual, larger drama-performance at Gene fornby. Dramas of sagas have, however, since the start of rebuilding the longhouse in 1990, been a natural part of the activities and daily life of the site and are an integral part of meeting tourists, schoolchildren and so on. At Gene fornby a "family" has been made up (a chieftain, his wife, children, maids, grandmother and so on) over the years and this family has identifiable individuals, all with their own names and different personalities. People who frequently work at Gene fornby have personified these characters during the years, some of them totally identifying with their roll so fully that it is impossible to change them and get another person to take over that specific roll.

Every year the story of the Gene family develops as a new play is written for every summer season. That means that the saga tradition develops and goes on every year in a "created" saga. This created history makes the whole Gene farm alive and it is the people in the play, many of them working at Gene during the summer season, that make the farm alive with their own stories and personalities.

## Other historical sites in the region

**Arnäsbacken-** remains of a settlement used from the Merovingian Period till the end of the Medieval Period about 10 kilometres north of Örnsköldsvik. Swedens northernmost graveyard with several grave-mounds.

**Bjästamon-** newly excavated area about 30 kilometres south of Örnsköldsvik. Archaeologists found remains of houses and activities from Stone Age until late age. The first found Stone Age village in the northern part of Sweden.

**Nämforsen-** One of the most known and best-preserved places of Stone Age rock carvings in Scandinavia. About 150 kilometres from Örnsköldsvik. *www.namforsen.com*

**Styresholm Medieval village-** A partly reconstructed medieval area by river Ångermanälven. Situated about 100 kilometres south of Örnsköldsvik.

### Literature about Gene
Lena Edblom: *Långhuset i Gene- Ett treskeppigt järnåldershus och dess konstruktion.* Umeå 1997.

Lena Edblom: *Stuga och Säte- Rum och inredning i ett järnåldershus.* Umeå 2002.

Lena Edblom: *Långhus i Gene- Teori och praktik i rekonstruktion.* Studia Archaeologica Universitatis Umensis 18. Umeå 2004.

Anna-Karin Lindqvist, Per H. Rahmqvist: *Gene. En stormansgård från äldre järnålder i Mellannorrland.* HB Prehistorica 1993.

Per H. Ramqvist, *Gene.* Archaeology and Environment 1. Umeå 1983.

### Further information
*www.ornskoldsvik.se/genefornby*
*www.ornskoldsvik.se/turism*
*www.mittsverigeturism.se*

*The broch of Mousa seems to have been a favourite spot for run away lovers. It was used by a young couple fleeing from Norway in Egil's Saga who were actually married there. In a Shetland context however it is perhaps best remembered for the elopement of Erlend the Young and Margaret the mother of Earl Harald Maddadarson who took up residence in the broch until Harald arrived to break up their romantic interlude. The story does have a happy ending however since the couple were subsequently married.*

# The Shetland Islands

## On the borderline

The Shetland Islands are situated on the borderline between the Atlantic Ocean and the North Sea some 300km or so to the North of Scotland and almost the same distance to the West of Norway. This location has encouraged seafarers from many periods to stop at the islands and to use them not only as a base but also as a "refuelling" stop for taking on fresh supplies and fresh crewmembers. For a long period the most common sailors around the islands were from Scandinavia and Shetland still retains many place names and cultural characteristics inherited from the islands "Viking "past. Indeed the kings of Norway controlled Shetland until well into the 15th century and the relatively remote nature of the islands has allowed them to retain much of their Norse culture despite the best efforts a succession of Scots overlords. A Scandanavian language (Norn) was commonly spoken until well into

*Geilsahellir a possible site for the giant lair in Geitishamrar.*

*Photo: Eileen Brooke Freeman*

the 18th Century and traces of this can even now be found in the distinctive Shetland dialect still used by native islanders. This is nowhere more apparent than in the islands' stories and legends which reflect not only the influence and prevalence of Norse settlers but also their beliefs and superstitions.

## Fljotsdala Saga

The Fljotdala Saga deals largely with the lives of the people of the Fljotsdal area in Iceland and in particular with the descendants of Thidrandi the Old. However one of Thidrandi's sons, Thorvald, has an adventurous trip to Shetland where he kills a giant with a magic sword, rescues a princess, marries her and subsequently takes her (and her mother!) home to Iceland. The story is a wonderful small vignette in a much longer and more involved tale and deserves a wider readership. The exact location of Thorvald's adventures has long been the object of extensive debate. There is a very clear description of the area and the spot is even named as Geitishamar with a nearby hill called Geitissulur but unfortunately there is no corresponding place name on modern maps. The current best guess at the location is on the island of Yell at a place near to West Sandwick which is called Geilsahellir and which matches in many regards the description it the text.

## Orkneyinga Saga

The Orkneyinga Saga has a number of references to Shetland since the Earldom that provides the basis of the narrative comprised

*Mousa Broch a favourite spot for eloping lovers.*
Photo: David Cooper

both Orkney and Shetland for much of its history and one of the most famous stories from the Orkneyinga to feature Shetland is the use of Mousa Broch by Erlend Ungi and Margaret Hakonsdottar as a hiding place when fleeing from Earl Harald Maddadson.

Even more important is the story of the use of the islands as a base by Earl Rognvald Kali Kolsson when pressing his claim for the Earldom. For at least part of the time Earl Rognvald made his main base of operations at Yell Sound although there is no clear indication as to the exact spot along this coast where he may have stayed. He, or more correctly his father Kol, made use of subterfuge to ensure that a warning beacon set up on Fair Isle was never lit so that his rival for the earldom had no warning of his arrival in Orkney. This allowed Rognvald to establish a strong foothold on the island of Westray and contributed greatly to the success of his campaign.

*Yell Sound where Rognvald's ships were stolen by Earl Paul.*
Photo: David Cooper

Rognvald was later shipwrecked on the islands on his way back from Norway and stayed in the south end of Shetland for some time where the story of the hooded man originated. This story, which involves a fishing expedition to from Sumburgh and around Horse Island also has Earl Rognvald appearing amongst his subjects incognito. Such stories are of course common in many cultures and it is interesting that it should appear in a Shetland context as part of the Scandinavian heritage.

## Unst Stories

The island of Unst has long been known for its Viking connections as evidenced by the extensive numbers of longhouse sites on the island. It is equally well provided for in terms of Viking folklore and stories. King Harald Fairhair was said to have landed at Haroldswick on the island when he made his voyage to Shetland to clear out Vikings who were raiding the Norwegian coast as mentioned in Heimskringla and indeed local legend has him buried there in a location called, naturally enough, Harald's Grave. That this conflicts strongly with all documentary evidence to the contrary has never been allowed to spoil a good story.

Local legend also has it that the Danish sea king Guthrum, scourge of Alfred the Great and conqueror of half of England, was trapped in a cave on the island on his way to invade Britain. His rescue by a local chieftain's daughter and later rewarding of her for the service forms the basis of a highly entertaining tale whose veracity is supported by the existence of a cave named Gotrum's Hole in a cliff face on the North West corner of the isle. Some versions of this story also indicated that Guthrum assembled at least part of his fleet in Yell Sound before departing on his English adventure.

*Sumburgh where Rognvald Kali Kolsson once fished.* Photo: David Cooper

One of the last Viking stories set in Shetland also had its origins in Unst. Set in the transition period between Norse and Scottish rule this is the tale of a delegation of Norse farmers who defied their new Scottish masters and sailed to the Scottish mainland to lay their case directly before the king. The Scottish laird at that period was Laurence Bruce who resided in Muness Castle and had a grim reputation for the subjection of these free men who had largely governed themselves under the Norse system. The story is interwoven with tragic deaths and forbidden love to add to an already explosive situation. It is relatively rare for folk tales in Shetland to have such an obvious political origin but this perhaps reflects the deep resentment which many freemen felt at that time regarding the loss of their independence.

## Fetlar Stories

Fetlar is reckoned by some to have been the first landfall of the Vikings in Shetland. It

*The Giant's Grave.* Photo: David Cooper

*Thorvald son of Thidrandi prepares to battle a giant.*                    *Drawing: David Cooper*

unfortunate Norwegian fisherman who is blown across the North Sea and dies on the island but only after rewarding the islanders who attempted to rescue him with the location of a marvellous fishing ground. The Giant's Grave is said to have marked his internment and recent excavations have all but proved that there was indeed a boat burial at the spot.

## Girlsta

The name Girlsta Water has its origins explained in another Viking story about an explorer on his way to a great island in the far north. Legend has it that a man called Flokki set off from Norway to find a great

has certainly long been the home of legendary storytellers and has a number of stories that have become standards in the Shetland storytelling scene. The most famous of these is undoubtedly about Jan Teit, a Fetlar resident of Viking times, and the bear he is given to look after by the King of Norway. It is perhaps an over simplification to say that he was "given" the bear as in truth he was forced to capture and keep the creature as punishment for killing one of the king's tax collectors. The bear ended its life captive on the island of Linga and the "Bears Bate" or path that it wore in the ground can still be spotted on aerial photos of the island to this day.

Also associated with a spot in Fetlar is the story of The Giant's Grave that tells of an

*Geirhilda daughter of Flokki of the Ravens.*
*Drawing: David Cooper*

island to the north but he was unsure of how to get there having only been as far as Faeroes before. He stopped off at Shetland and while he was there he raided a raven's nest and stole three young ravens. The ravens took their revenge and when he returned to his ship he discovered that his daughter Geirhilda had been tragically drowned in the nearby lake which was afterwards called Geirhildasvatn which has been corrupted to Girlsta Water. Flokki continued with his journey and after leaving the Faeroe Islands he released a raven each day. The first two flew back towards Faeroe but the third flew onwards and guided him to the land he was seeking. Flokki of the Ravens, as he became known, settled in an area of fjords and mountains later to be called the Westfjords and is credited with giving the land its name of Iceland.

## Creature Stories

Trows are the "hidden people" of Shetland folklore and there has long been a belief that Norse settlers created them as a means of weaving the Pictish former residents of the islands into their stories. This would tend to be supported by the alternative title for these often grim little creatures which was Pechts. Whether it is true or not there are certainly plenty of trowie stories around many of which are of ancient origin. The trows were small dark and mysterious. They lived underground in "trowie knowes", which we now recognise as burnt mounds or burial mounds, and could be mischievous, cruel or kind depending on how they were treated by their human neighbours.

One of the most famous of trowie stories is about the disruption to the building of an

*Girlsta Water burial site of Geirhilda.*

*Photo: David Cooper*

*Pettawater, the lake of the pechts or trows.*                    *Photo: David Cooper*

early Christian church in Uyeasound in Unst known as the Glatnakirk. It tells the story of an early Christian missionary's encounter with the trows the results of which could perhaps best be described as a score draw with the trows having the best of the play but the missionary scoring a last minute equaliser. The Magical well of Yela Brun was also said to be a result of this tale.

Another trow story relates to the formation of the loch of Pettawater and a sharp depression in the nearby hill called K'neefel. This story involves a luckless giant who tries to capture a tribe of trows who are tormenting him with the intention of carrying them to Norway. Alas they escape his clutches and he eventually moves to Norway himself to get away from them. Pettawater is probably a corruption of Pechtisvater. (Water of the Picts)

Along with the trows Shetland also had its share of giants in Norse times and the most famous of these were Herma and Saxa who gave their names to the headlands in Unst called Hermaness and Saxaford along with a few other places such as Herman's Ha, Saxa's Ba and Saxa's Kettle. These argumentative giants were a very competitive pair and eventually lost their lives competing for the love of a fair mermaid. Both drowned in an attempt to race to the North Pole and doubtless their bone still lie undisturbed just beyond the edge of the continental shelf.

## Further information

*www.shetland-heritage.co.uk*
*www.shetlandtourism.com*
*www.visitshetland.com*

*He [earl Magnus] fell upon the earth and commended himself to God, offering himself as a sacrifice. Not only did he prey for himself and his friends, but also for his enemies and murderers, and forgave from the bottom of his heart those who had done him evil. [...] After that he crossed himself, and bowed himself to the stroke; and he was struck in the middle of the head with a single blow, and so passed from the world to God.*

(From the Orkneyinga Saga)

# The Orkney Islands and the Orkneyinga Saga

## Introduction

The Orkney Islands are a group of around 70 islands that lie off the northernmost tip of Scotland. These islands are rightly famous for their archaeological sites, including many well preserved houses, tombs and standing stones dating from the Stone Age. The green, fertile islands soon proved to be an irresistible lure for Viking settlers who started to arrive in the late 8th century AD, gaining control of Orkney and giving the islands their place names. Orkney may also have been used by Vikings as a strategically important place to raid from, as its geographical position gave easy access to the seas around the east and west coasts of Britain and Ireland. Lying at the crossroads

*St Magnus Cathedral, Kirkwall, Orkney.*

*Photo: Raymond Parks*

*Maeshowe tomb, Stenness, Orkney.*

*Photo: Agne Säterberg*

between the Celtic and Nordic worlds, Orkney soon became the powerbase for an earldom that extended from the Northern Isles of Orkney and Shetland, through a large part of northern Scotland, the Hebrides and even into Ireland. Although the title of earl was granted by the king of Norway, the earls of Orkney often paid little heed to their rulers and acted independently. Over the centuries the influence of Scotland and its kings spread to the islands around its coast. The end of Scandinavian rule came in 1468 when Orkney was pawned to the Scottish crown by King Christian I of Denmark in lieu of a dowry for his daughter, Margaret, on her marriage to King James III of Scotland. Shetland would share the same fate

the following year. Although these islands are no longer ruled by a Nordic country, the dialect, culture and spirit of its people has more in common with Scandinavia that Scotland.

## The Sagas

Orkney appears in several sagas, sometimes it is just a passing mention, but there are other important saga references that give us a valuable insight into life in Viking age Orkney. The main saga relating to Orkney is the *Orkneyinga Saga* (The Saga of the Orkney Islanders), which tells the story of the earls of Orkney from the years c874 - 1214. It tells of an expedition to Shetland

..... "mæth thæiri ohse er ate Koukr Trænilsonr fyrir sunan lant."
.. with the axe which belonged to Gauk Trandilsson in the South of Iceland.

*Runic inscription in Maeshowe tomb.*                    Photo: Agne Säterberg

and Orkney by King Harald Fair-hair around the year 874 to subdue Vikings who were attacking Norway. During this voyage his loyal follower, Earl Rognvald of More, was given Orkney and Shetland as compensation for the death of one of his sons. It was from Rognvald that the earls of Orkney were descended. This expedition by King Harald Fair-hair appears in several sagas, but there is no documentary evidence from either Britain or Ireland to support the claim.

Earl Sigurd the Stout of Orkney was killed at the Battle of Clontarf, near Dublin in Ireland in the year 1014. He carried a magic banner at the head of his army that was embroidered with the image of a raven in flight. This banner brought victory to the army that carried it before them, but death to the standard-bearer who held it. Earl Sigurd died after he was forced to conceal the banner under his clothes, as no one else would carry it. The *Orkneyinga Saga* tells us little about Earl Sigurd, but other sagas fill the gaps. *Gunnlaugs Saga Ormstunga* (The Saga of Gunnlaug Serpent-Tongue) tells how the Icelandic poet Gunnlaug was well rewarded for composing a poem in honour of Earl Sigurd. In Vatnsdæla Saga (The Saga of the People of Vatnsdal) Thorkel Scratcher, a kinsman of Earl Sigurd, spends time at Sigurd's court and goes raiding with him. In *Þorstein's Saga Síðu-Hallssonar* (Thorstein Sidu-Hallsson's Saga) Thorstein goes raiding with Earl Sigurd, and fights in his army at the Battle of Clontarf. The saga that tells us the most about Sigurd and his death is *Brennu-Njáls Saga* (Njal's Saga). Two of

Njal's sons had been warriors at Earl Sigurd's court, while in a strange twist of fate their killers would later replace them. The Battle of Clontarf was accompanied by strange supernatural omens, including the valkeries (Odin's handmaidens) being seen weaving human guts on a loom made from spears, while using arrows and swords as shuttles and weaving battons, and human heads as weights. They chanted a magical song as they wove this web of war; directing the battle and the fate of those who fought in it.

*Ring of Brodgar, a Neolithic stone circle, Stenness, Orkney.*          *Photo: Agne Säterberg*

Other versions of the *Orkneyinga Saga* can be found in the *Flatyjarbók* (Flatey (island) Book) and a short account in *Heimskringla* (The Saga of the Kings of Norway). Earl Harald Maddadsson's loss of Shetland in 1194 is told in *Sverri's Saga* (The Saga of King Sverri). The final expedition west from Norway was made by King Hakon Hakonsson in 1263, as told in Hakonar Saga (The Saga of King Hakon). After defeat at the Battle of Largs in Scotland he returned to Orkney where he died in the Bishop's Palace in Kirkwall.

## The locations

It would be impossible to list all of the places mentioned in the *Orkneyinga Saga*, as virtually the whole of Orkney is the stage on which the saga is played out. What are listed below are the major sites that have saga connections, and date from that period. You can visit them, touch them and marvel in the fact that you are walking in the footsteps of the Vikings.

**The Brough of Deerness** is a small island connected to the East Mainland parish of Deerness. It can be accessed by a flight of

*Brough of Deerness.*                    *Copyright: Orkney Library and Archive*

modern stone steps down the cliff face, then by a narrow path up the side of the island itself. On the Brough lie the remains of a Norse chapel, surrounded by longhouses. Only the chapel has been excavated, showing it to have been a later stone structure that replaced an earlier timber building.

The nearby farm of Skaill may have been the site of the hall that belonged to Thorkel Fosterer, the foster-father of Earl Thorfinn the Mighty (c1009-1065). It was in this hall that Thorkel killed Earl Thorfinn's half-brother, Earl Einar Wry-mouth. Thorkel and Earl Einar were mortal enemies, but they were brought to terms and each had to prepare a feast for the other. Earl Einar visited Thorkel, but was in a sour mood during his stay. When they were supposed to ride to Earl Einar's hall for the return feast, Thorkel has spies travel the route they were

about to take. They reported armed men in ambush waiting to kill Thorkel, so he casually walked up to Earl Einar and struck him on the head with his sword, killing him instantly.

A magnificent Norse church with twin circular towers once stood next to the farm of Skaill, but sadly it was demolished to make way for a new parish church in 1798. There is a red sandstone hogback grave marker inside the church. It probably dates from the 12th century. These triangular blocks of red sandstone are carved to look like a tiled roof and lay over the graves of important people. The parish of Deerness is connected to the rest of the Mainland by a thin strip of sand. It is here that a mound called Dingieshowe was used by the Vikings to hold their regional parliamentary gatherings. It was during one of these gatherings that Thorkel Fosterer made an enemy of Earl Einar Wry-mouth, which would ultimately lead to Earl Einar's murder.

**St Olaf's Kirk** was built in Kirkwall by Earl Rognvald Brusisson in the late 1030s, and dedicated to his foster-father, St Olaf (the former king of Norway). Earl Rognvald ruled Orkney with his uncle Thorfinn the Mighty for several years before they fell out over land. Rognvald had tried to kill Thorfinn by burning him in his hall, but he escaped. Thorfinn would later burn the house that Rognvald was staying in, but he too escaped by leaping over the heads of his attackers as they stood in the doorway. He hid among the rocks by the shore, but was betrayed by the barking of his lapdog and killed. Nothing now remains of the original church, which was replaced by a stone structure in the 16th century. An archway from this later building can still be seen in St Olaf's Wynd.

**St Magnus Cathedral** in Kirkwall is by far the most spectacular building from the period of the Norse earls of Orkney. The red sandstone cathedral was founded in 1137 by Earl Rognvald Kali Kolsson in honour of his martyred uncle, St Magnus. It has been altered on many occasions. The early Romanesque arches with their rounded tops can bee seen in the central part of the building, while the later Gothic arches with their pointed tops can be seen at either end of the building. Pilgrims would visit the shrine of St Magnus, bringing money and power to the church and to the town of Kirkwall. Earl Rognvald Kali would be

canonised in the late 12th century, meaning there were the remains of two saints in the cathedral. Their bones were found in two pillars in the cathedral in the 19th and 20th centuries, and they remain there to this day. It is possible that the bones were secretly hidden at the time of the Reformation to prevent their destruction. St Magnus cathedral is still used as a church, as well as a venue for concerts.

**The Bishop's Palace** is situated across the road from St Magnus Cathedral. What you see now (including the large round tower) actually dates from the 16th century, but the core of the building goes back to the foundation of the cathedral in 1137. It was built for Bishop William the Old, the first bishop of St Magnus Cathedral. It was in this building that King Hakon Hakonsson died

*Interior of the Bishop's Palace in Kirkwall, Orkney.* *Photo: Raymond Parks*

during Yule in 1263. He was temporarily buried in the cathedral before his body was exhumed in the spring of 1264 and taken back to Norway for burial in Bergen.

**The Orkney Museum** is situated across the road from the cathedral in Tankerness House, a laird's townhouse dating from the 16ᵗʰ century. It contains galleries on the Vikings and Medieval Orkney. Artefacts on display include a whale bone plaque carved with two dragons' heads that was found in a Viking boat burial from Scar in Sanday, and the simple wooden box that once contained the bones of St Magnus.

**Maeshowe** is the largest and grandest of the Stone Age tombs that can still be visited in Orkney. It was broken into more than once during the period of Norse rule in Orkney. The *Orkneyinga Saga* records one such incident in 1153, when Earl Harald

Maddadsson and his men sought shelter from a snow storm in 'Orkahaugr,' as it was known. One of the earl's men went mad during the night as a result of staying in the tomb. Evidence of Norse activity can be seen all over the inside of the tomb, as they cut runic graffiti into the ancient stones. It is the largest collection of runic inscriptions outside Scandinavia, and includes depictions of animals, including the beautiful 'Maeshowe Dragon.'

**The Earl's Bu** in Orphir was once an important residence of the earls of Orkney. The nearby round church, dedicated to St Nicholas, is thought to have been built by Earl Hakon Paulsson following a pilgrimage to the Holy Land after the murder in c1116 of his co-ruler and cousin, Earl Magnus (later St Magnus). This round church, unique in Scotland, was complete until 1757 when it was partially demolished to make way for a

*St Nicholas church at the Earl's Bu, Orphir Orkney.*          *Photo: Raymond Parks*

*Brough of Birsay, Orkney.*                    *Photo: Raymond Parks*

new parish church (itself now demolished). Near the church lie the remains of buildings, including part of a Norse watermill.

**The Brough of Birsay** is a tidal island off the West Mainland parish of Birsay. Here can be seen the remains of buildings dating from the 9ᵗʰ - 12ᵗʰ centuries. A church dedicated to St Peter dates to the later period of use, as do the monastic buildings next to it. Earlier Viking longhouses lie on the upper slopes of the site, which in turn was built on an existing Pictish settlement. Earl Thorfinn the Mighty had his hall in Birsay, but it was probably in the village on the Mainland opposite the Brough. Thorfinn built a cathedral in Birsay, dedicated to Christ, which is thought to lie near the present St Magnus Kirk. It was in Christ Kirk that St Magnus was buried after his murder on Egilsay in c1116. His bones were later removed to St Olaf Kirk in Kirkwall after he

appeared in a vision to a Westray farmer and ordered it to be done.

**Eynhallow** is a small island that lies between the Mainland and the island of Rousay. A well preserved 12ᵗʰ century church can be seen, surrounded by later buildings. The opportunity of visiting the island is strictly limited to one special trip every July.

**The Wirk** on the island of Rousay was probably the home of the 12ᵗʰ century chieftain Sigurd of Westness. All that can be seen now is the remains of a square tower partially obscured by the build up of soil washed down from the steep hillside. It was while staying with Sigurd of Westness that Earl Paul the Silent was kidnapped by the chieftain Svein Asleifsson in 1136 as he and his men hunted otters by the cliffs. He was carried south to exile and ultimately to his death, leaving the way clear for Rognvald

*Orkney fiddle player Ruby Manson joining in with a fiddle tune played by Naja Illeris from Greenland, at Kirbuster.*                                                                    Photo: Agne Säterberg

Kali Kolsson to claim the earldom. Next to the Wirk is the well preserved **St Mary's Kirk**, which also dates from the 12th century. A picturesque walk from this site leads to Westness, the site of an earlier Viking cemetery.

**Cubbie Roo's Castle** on the neighbouring island of Wyre is the remains of the 12th century stronghold of the local chieftain, Kolbein Hruga. He was said to be a huge man, and became associated with the boulder throwing Orkney giant Cubbie Roo. This castle, complete with ditches and ramparts, was a place of refuge in times of trouble. The main hall was probably under the neighbouring farm called the Bu. **St Mary's Kirk** lies below the slope

of the castle, and dates from the late 12th century. This well preserved church may have been built by Kolbein, or his son Bishop Bjarni.

**St Magnus Kirk** on the island of Egilsay dates from the 12th century and is dedicated to Earl Magnus Erlendsson who was murdered on the island by his cousin Earl Hakon. He had ruled peacefully with Hakon for many years, until Hakon's supporters stirred up trouble between them. A peace meeting was arranged to be held on Egilsay during Easter sometime around the year 1116. Magnus set off with two longships, as they had agreed, but as they crossed the calm sea a wave rose out of nowhere and broke over Magnus. He declared that this was a bad

*Cubbie Roo's Castle, Wyre, Orkney.*
Photo: Gunnie Moberg

omen, and that his life would soon be at an end. His followers begged him to return home, but he refused. Hakon arrived with eight longships and a band of fully armed warriors. They captured Magnus and had him put to death. Hakon had been tempted to have him maimed and imprisoned, but the local chieftains said that they would no longer accept the rule of two earls, so Hakon ordered Magnus's death. His standard bearer refused to do the killing, so it fell to Lifolf the cook to carry out the murder. Magnus asked that he should be struck on the head with the axe rather than beheaded like a common criminal. A memorial erected in 1937 marks the spot where local tradition says the martyrdom of St Magnus took place. The fine church with its tall round tower was not built until after Magnus's death, and is dedicated to the Orkney saint.

**Cross Kirk** on the island of Westray dates from the 12th century, and was probably built by Thorkel Flayer, a local chieftain.

Excavations at a nearby site found a high status building dating from the same period, which supports the theory that this was the church that went with the Chieftain's hall. Thorkel was alive at the time that Earl Rognvald Kali Kolsson's invasion fleet arrived at Pierowall in 1136. He had arrived unexpectedly, as he had used a spy to sabotage the beacon on Fair Isle between Orkney and Shetland. It was too wet to light and so warn Earl Paul the Silent that Rognvald's invasion fleet was on its way from Shetland. Rognvald seized power, and was responsible for the building of St Magnus cathedral in Kirkwall in honour of his saintly uncle.

**St Boniface Kirk** on the island of Papa Westray was built in the 12th century. For many years it served as the local parish church before falling into disrepair. It was lovingly restored in the late 20th century. In the graveyard outside is a 12th century hogback gravestone. Earl Rognvald Brusisson was buried on Papa Westray after he was killed during a dispute over land with his uncle, Earl Thorfinn the Mighty. Although St Boniface Kirk was built a century after Rognvald's death it may have replaced an earlier church that once stood on the same site.

## Further information
*www.visitorkney.com*
*www.orkney.gov.uk*

*After sailing from Dublin via the Hebrides, Caithness, Orkney and the Faroes Aud the Deep-
Minded, widow of a Viking King in Dublin, made her home at Hvamm in Western Iceland. She
used to say prayers at Kross Hills and had crosses erected there, for she'd been baptized and was a
devout Christian.*

(From the Book of Settlement)

The Isle of Man has so many spectacular sites of interest from the Viking Age that the whole island is a highlight on any Viking trail. The Island is mentioned in many of the great sagas, from Njal's, the Orkneyinga, Heimskringla, the Saga of Eiric the Red and the poetic Eddas. Still rich in folklore, there is plenty of evidence of sagas and storytelling on this Isle. All parts of the Island are easily accessible either by car or by bus.

## The Sound

Njal's Saga, the longest Icelandic saga, is a complex tale of wisdom and revenge. The Sound, at the southern most tip of the

*Aerial view of the Sound and the Calf of Man.*

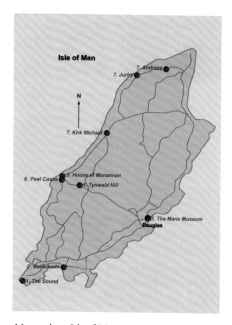

*Map to how Isle of Man.*
*Copyright: Manx National Heritage*

was haunted by dreadful visions and blood-curdling noises.  Ospak interpreted these as bad omens.  In spite of Brodir's plan to kill Ospak and his men by blocking them in the Sound, Ospak predicted this and he and his ships slipped away under the cover of night and sailed to warn and assist King Brian.

The Sound today is a haven for wildlife and the visions and sounds are from far more natural sources - the birds and the seals.  There is a recently developed café and heritage centre at the Sound where visitors can learn about the area and maybe imagine the presence of Brodir's ships and visions!

## Balladoole

The sagas are packed with noble and honourable deaths and on Isle of Man, in the 9th century AD, a pagan Viking was laid to rest in a boat burial at Balladoole. Looking out over the sea and land, stones set in the shape of the ship can be seen on the top of the low hill today, marking the burial place of a warrior-farmer.  Artefacts including the remains of a shield, harness mounts, stirrups, buckles and a cloak pin show influences from Scotland and Ireland.  These artefacts are on display at the Manx Museum.

Prehistoric flints, Bronze Age burials, Iron Age earthworks, Early Christian lintel graves (slate coffins) and a chapel have also been revealed at Balladoole.

Balladoole is a Listed Ancient Monument in the care of Manx National Heritage and is accessible on foot.

*Open site. Unsupervised access at all times.*

Island, features in this saga, often thought of as the greatest of them all.  Sigtrygg, from Ireland, on a mission to kill King Brian, king of Ireland, sought help from Earl Sigurd in Orkney.  His help would come at the Battle of Clontarff in exchange for the kingdom and Sigtrygg's mother.  However, more help would be needed and it was to the Vikings Ospak and Brodir, their ships lying off the Isle of Man, that Sigtrygg also turned.  Offering the same prizes, the kingdom and his mother, Sigtrygg won the support of Brodir - a Christian turned sorcerer, whose black hair was so long that it was tucked into his belt!  But Ospak refused to help and drew up his 10 ships inside the Sound.  Brodir anchored his 20 ships outside the Sound, but

*Aerial view of Balladoole - stones mark the site of the boat burial.*

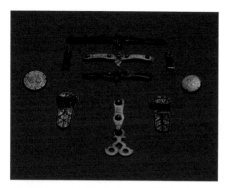

*Horse harness pieces - Balladoole Viking burial.*
Copyright: Manx National Heritage

*Tynwald Hill.*
Copyright: Manx National Heritage

## The Manx Museum

"Thie Tashtee Vannin" - the Treasure House of Man - has a wealth of information on the time of the sagas, but also introduces "The Story of Mann", developed by Manx National Heritage to promote an integrated approach to the rich cultural and natural heritage of the Isle of Man.

The Viking gallery displays artefacts from the time of Norse occupancy - from hoards of silver to fragments of woollen cloaks. There is a section devoted to the art of the Manx carved crosses and replicas, many of which depict scenes from Norse myth and legend. With characters such as Loki, the catalyst for Ragnarok, Sigurd roasting the serpent Fafni's heart and Odin being devoured by Fenris the wolf at Ragnarok, the Manx stones help bring the stories to life. The use of replicas enable the intricate designs to be outlined and help to explain these complex monuments.

Information and further details of access to sites throughout the Island can be obtained at *www.gov.im/mnh*

## Tynwald

The parliament site, Tynwald, is in the tradition of the Viking Age Thing sites, where justice was administered and stories shared; the Tyn element is a corruption of the word Thing. Here, the modern Parliament still meets on the 5th July each year for the ceremony where new laws are proclaimed. The site is easily accessible.

## The House of Manannan

Using state-of-the-art display techniques, The House of Manannan at Peel explores the Celtic, Viking and Maritime traditions of the Isle of Man. This exploration of themes essential to Manx culture was declared British Isles Museum Of the Year 98/99.

Re-created sights, sounds and smells bring the Celtic and Viking worlds to life. Visitors can experience living in a Viking long house and listen to the conversation between a Viking settler and his native wife. Discussing

*The House of Manannan scene inside the Viking longhouse.*     Copyright: Manx National Heritage

their own gods and languages, this display gives an insight into how people from different cultures were able to interact. There is also an evocative display to help the visitor discover the legends depicted on the Manx crosses.

The vessels that carried the stories can be experienced too - Vikings can be seen unloading a ship, Odin's Raven - a two thirds scale replica of the Gokstad ship which was built and sailed from Norway to the Isle of Man in 1979. Events during the period of Viking rule on the Isle of Man can be discovered through the "Chronicles of the Kings of Man and the Isles".

## St Patrick's Isle, Peel

The 11th century ruling seat of the Norse Kingdom of Man and the Isles, first united by Godred Crovan is at Peel Castle. One of the Isle of Man's principle historic monuments, this fortress occupies the important site of St Patrick's Isle at Peel.

The Castle's curtain wall encircles the ruins of many buildings which are a testimony to the site's religious and secular importance in Manx History.

The importance of the Isle as a centre for Manx Christianity was established in the 6th century and this role was to survive the arrival of the "pagan" Norse Vikings at the end of the 8th century. But recent excavations at St Patrick's Isle, have also revealed rich pagan graves. The most dramatic find was the Norse-period grave of a lady of high social status; the jewellery and effects buried with her can be seen on display with other excavation finds in the Manx Museum.

## Carved Stones

Since the 5th century AD crosses have served in the Isle of Man as grave markers and memorial stones. After the Vikings settled on Mann, and later converted to Christianity, Norse sculptors decorated their stones with images from their pagan mythology. It is these stones more than any other monument that provide illustrations of the characters and events from the sagas. Many of the stones can still be viewed in the parish of their discovery.

In the north, at Andreas, Thorwald's cross depicts the moment at Ragnarok when Odin is devoured by Fenris the wolf. On the other side of the same stone, a figure is shown with a cross and book, perhaps denoting the move away from the pagan past to Christianity.

At Jurby, amongst the outstanding examples is a depiction of what has been interpreted as Heimdall, Warder of the Gods, blowing the Giallar-horn - heralding the coming of Ragnarok.

*Aerial view of Peel Castle.*

*Copyright: Manx National Heritage*

*Heimdall Cross, Jurby.*
Copyright: Manx National Heritage

There are many crosses preserved in the parish church at Kirk Michael, but one that draws attention is Grim's cross. With illustrations of bird-headed men, this has been interpreted as depicting Valhalla, even showing the great fish which swims through the stream.

Crosses can be seen at the following parish churches;

St Andrew's Church, Andreas
St Patrick's Church, Jurby
St Bridget's Church, Bride
St Maughold's Church, Maughold
St Michael's Church, Kirk Michael
St Adamnan's Church, Lonan
St Peter's, Onchan
St Braddan's Old Church, Braddan

*Open sites.  Unsupervised access at all times.*

## Further information

*www.gov.im/mnh*
*www.gov.im/tourism*

*Thorwald's Cross showing Odin and Fenris wolf.*
Copyright: Manx National Heritage

*One morning, as spring advanced, they noticed a large number of hide-covered boats rowing boats [...]. There were so many of them that it looked as if bits of coal had been tossed over the water, and there was a pole waving from each boat. They signalled with their shields and began trading with the visitors [natives], who mostly wished to trade for red cloth.*
(From Eirik the Red's Saga)

## L'Anse aux Meadows
## National Historic Site of Canada

## The Vinland sagas

The Saga of the Greenlanders tells about a young Icelander, Bjarni Herjolfsson, who, in the year 985 or 986, saw thitherto unknown coasts south and west of Greenland when he lost his course en route from Iceland to his father's new home in southwestern Greenland. His discoveries caused great excitement in Greenland, but the colony,

which had just been established that year, needed time to get on its feet before they could afford further exploration. Around the year 1000 the time had come. The man to lead the new venture was Leif, son of the founder and paramount chief of the Greenland colony, Erik the Red. Leif retraced Bjarni's steps, setting sail west across Davis Strait. His first landing was in an inhospitable area where land consisted mostly

*Vast forests cover central Labrador, Pinware.*                    Photo: B. Wallace.

*Caribou in Helluland.*                                                   Photo: Rolf Hicker

of slabs of rock, mountains and glaciers. He gave the land a name and called it *Helluland*, Land of Rock Slabs.

From Helluland, he continued south for two days. At that point, he landed in a more level area with vast woods extending almost to the sandy shores. This land he named *Markland*, Land of Forests. From there he continued south with a northeasterner for another two days and then, according the Saga of the Greenlanders:

*...they saw land. They sailed towards it and came to an island, which lay to the north of the land, where they went ashore. In the fine weather they found dew on the grass, that they collected in their hands and drank, and thought they had never tasted anything so sweet.*
*    Afterwards they returned to their ship and sailed into the sound which lay between the island and the headland that stretched out*
*northwards from the land. They rounded the headland and steered westward. ..*
*    ...they carried their sleeping-sacks ashore and built booths. Later they decided to spend the winter there and built large houses.*
*    It seemed to them the land was so good that livestock would need no fodder during the winter. The temperature never dropped below freezing, and the grass only weathered very slightly. The days and nights were much more equal in length than in Greenland and Iceland. In the depth of winter the sun was aloft by mid-morning and still visible at mid-afternoon.*
*    When they had finished building their houses, Leif spoke to his companions: >I want to divide our company into two groups, as I wish to explore the land. One half is to remain at home by the longhouses, [halls]  while the other half explores the land. They are never to go any farther than will enable them to return that same evening and no one is to separate from the group...Leif was a large, strong man, of very*

*striking appearance and wise, as well as being a man of moderation in all things* (Sagas of the Icelanders, 2000: 639-640).

Leif's establishment was called *Leifsbúðir*, Leif's Booth or Leif's Camp. A booth was a cross between a house and a tent. It had walls of sod and a roof of tent cloth held up with loose poles pitched on top of the walls. The Saga of the Greenlanders tells us that during these explorations, grapes were found and collected and the trees they grew were cut to provide a load of lumber to bring back to Greenland. The lumber was an important cargo as there were no forests in Greenland. The discovery of grapes was such a sensational find that Leif named this land Vínland, Land of Wine. Wine was a drink for chieftains, much cherished by the leaders of the community who regularly gave lavish banquets as a sign of their greatness.

After Leif's return to Greenland, five more expeditions were launched from Greenland to Leif's Camp. All were led by Leif's siblings or a relative. Leif no longer participated because he had assumed the chieftainship on the death of his father, but the expeditions required his authorization and he would have received a share of the profits made on the Vinland goods. One expedition never reached its goal but was tossed on the ocean an entire summer before it could make it back to Greenland. After the fifth expedition, Leif's Camp was abandoned. A contributing factor was the fact that the new lands were already occupied by large groups of people, and relations between them and the Norse were not peaceful. The chief factor, though, was the small size of the Greenland colony, only about 500 people in Leif's time, and the long distance from Vinland to Greenland. It was actually shorter and easier to sail to Norway where lumber and wine could be had, as well as many other products not available in Vinland.

The Saga of Erik the Red gives a slightly different version of the Vinland voyages. In it the Icelander Thorfinn Karlsefni is the hero. Thorfinn was the husband of Leif's

*Can butternuts lead you to Vinland? Butternuts and a piece of butternut wood found among the Norse artifacts show that the occupants of L'Anse aux Meadows visited areas where grapes grow wild.*
Photo: Arctic Studies Center, Smithsonian Institution, - Peter Harboldt

widowed sister-in-law Gudrid.  This account of the Vinland voyages was compiled to add luster to one of their descendants living in the 12th century.  For that reason it almost erases Leif Eriksson from the story, and his expedition plus all the others are combined into one led by Karlsefni.  Also the name Leifsbúðir is purged and replaced by two other names, *Straumfjord*, Fjord of Currents, and *Hóp*, Tidal Lagoon.  That said, the Saga of the Greenlanders has also tampered with the actual events.  If one reads it carefully, one can see that episodes have been compressed and that Leifsbúðir is a combination of both Straumfjord and Hóp. So in some aspects the Saga of Erik the Red is more truthful.  This is also, as we will see, born out by the archaeological evidence at L'Anse aux Meadows. The documentary evidence is complicated because there are two separate versions of the Saga of Erik the Red: the Skalholt Book and Hauk's Book. Although almost identical, they differ in small details such as in some names and nature descriptions.  A careful comparison of the two has shown that Hauk's book is the more correct one.  This may be because Hauk, who edited this version around 1306 to 1308, was himself a direct descendant of Thorfinn Karlsefni and Gudrid and may have drawn on family knowledge (Ólafur Halldórsson, "The Vinland Voyages" in Icelandic Sagas, Eddas, and Art, 1981, page 49.  New York: The Piermont Morgan Library).

In the Saga of Erik the Red, Straumfjord is a large base from which explorations in all directions are launched during the summer months.  Hóp is a summer camp a good distance south of Straumfjord.  It is here that grapes are harvested and lumber cut. According to Hauk's book, Hóp was occupied only during two summer months, the entire expedition returning to Straumfjord for the winter.

Karlsefni's route to Vinland was the same as that of Leif's. He first landed at Helluland, later at Markland.  After that they came to Straumfjord.  Straumfjord is described as a beautiful place:

*Inside the main replica building in L'Anse aux Meadows.*

Photo: Rögnvaldur Guðmundsson

*...they sailed onwards, until they reached a fjord cutting into the coast. They steered their ships into the fjord with an island near its mouth, where there were strong currents, and called the island Straumsey* (Island of Currents). *There were so many birds* (Hauk's Book says eiders) *there that they could hardly walk without stepping on eggs. They sailed up into the fjord, which they called Straumsfjord* [Fjord of Currents], *unloaded the cargo from the ships and began settling in.*

*They had brought all sorts of livestock with them and explored the land and its resources. There were mountains there* [Hauk's Book does not mention mountains], *and a pleasant landscape. They paid little attention to things other then exploring the land. The grass there grew tall.*

*They spent the winter there, and it was a harsh winter, for which they had made little preparation, and they grew short of food, and caught nothing when hunting or fishing. They*

*Fire strikers of Greenland jasper were found in the biggest hall, which had a floor space of more than 160 m² (where the main group is standing). Undoubtedly this is where the leader resided. Was this the hall built by Leif Eriksson?*

Photo: Rögnvaldur Guðmundsson

went out to the island, expecting to find some prey to hunt or food on the beaches. They found little food, but their livestock improved there... The weather improved so they could go fishing, and from then on they had supplies in plenty.

*In the spring they moved further into Straumfjord and lived on produce of both shores of the fjord: hunting game inland, gathering eggs on the island and fishing at sea* (Sagas of the Icelanders, 2000: 667-668).

Hóp was a bountiful place:
*They sailed a long time, until they came to a river which flowed into a lake and from there to the sea. There were white sandbars beyond the mouth of the river, and they could only sail into the river at high tide. Karlsefni and his company sailed into the lagoon and called the*

land Hop (Tidal Pool). *There they found fields of self-sown wheat in the low-lying areas and vines growing on the hills. Every stream was teeming with fish. They dug trenches along the high-water mark and when the tide ebbed there were halibut in them. There were a great number of deer of all kinds in the forest* (Sagas of the Icelanders, 2000: 669).

However, the Norse were not alone at Hóp. The area was inhabited by large groups of native people. At first there was a peaceful trade, the Norse offering red cloth (the Saga of the Greenlanders says milk) in return for furs. But soon a fight broke out. Eventually people were killed on both sides.
*The party then realized that, despite everything the land had to offer there, they would be under constant threat of attack from its prior*

*inhabitants. They made ready to depart for their own country*
(Sagas of the Icelanders, 2000: 671).

Although not forgotten, Vinland was abandoned, but trips to the closer places of Markland and Helluland for lumber and walrus ivory may have continued throughout the life of the Greenland colony.

## The site: L'Anse aux Meadows National Historic Site of Canada

L'Anse aux Meadows National Historic Site is part of a Canada-wide family of national parks, national historic sites, and national marine conservation areas.

### The Visitor Reception Centre

The Visitor Reception Centre features an exhibit of the archaeological evidence found on the site. The most important of the artifacts are prominently displayed in the main lobby. Details of the excavation and more artifacts as well as other Viking displays are in another room. There is also a film theatre showing a film, "Vinland Mystery" about Helge Ingstad's discovery of the site.

From the Visitor Reception Centre a board walk leads down to the archaeological remains of the Norse buildings, located about 350 metres from the Centre. There Interpreters conduct guided walking tours around the archaeological site and relate the story of the Norse in North America.

A short distance north of the ruins are four full-scale replicas of some of the buildings. Each summer interpreters, dressed in period Viking clothing re-enact what life may have been like at this base camp. The activities portrayed are based on the archaeological evidence uncovered from the original site.

L'Anse aux Meadows National Historic Site is open daily from early June to mid October.

### The Site of the Norse buildings

The ruins of the Norse buildings are located on a former beach terrace encircling a bog about 100 m in from the shore of Epaves Bay. The terrace is cut by a small brook, Black Duck Brook, issuing into the bay. Near its mouth is what remains of a small iron manufacture site where iron was produced in the New World for the first time. The rest of the buildings were dwellings, grouped into three complexes

*Over 600 Norse items were found in the bog adjacent to the buildings.*
Photo: R. Ferguson for Parks Canada

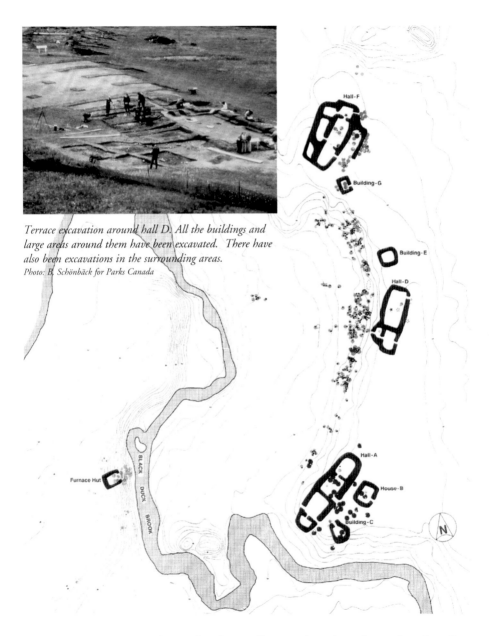

*Terrace excavation around hall D. All the buildings and large areas around them have been excavated. There have also been excavations in the surrounding areas.*
Photo: B. Schönbäck for Parks Canada

*Map of the site and the distribution of artifacts. Yellow is smelting slag, red is smithing slag. Green signifies carpentry waste, and blue discarded boat nails.*   Map: B. Galland and B. Wallace

located at even distances from each other. Each complex consists of a large hall flanked by a small hut. One of these complexes also has a small house next to the hall. The halls are very large. One spans over 100 square metres. This is double the space found in the hall owned by Erik the Red in Haukadal in Iceland. Another has many more rooms and measures over 160 square metres. Only chieftains and their entourage would have lived in such big buildings. Firestrikers of red jasper show that Greenlanders lived in the largest hall. This was probably the large house built by Leif Eriksson. Icelanders occupied the other two halls as here the firestrikers were of Icelandic jasper.

The architecture of all the buildings is distinctly Icelandic. The architectural details, the artifacts, and radiocarbon dates show that the buildings were inhabited around the year 1000. They also indicate that the occupation period was short, perhaps only a few years.

The layout of the site is unique among Norse sites. Barns and byres or other arrangements for domestic animals are missing, showing that the purpose of the site was not regular colonization. The artifacts indicate male activities such as carpentry, the making of iron, and boat repair, with little evidence of normal family life. The settlement was also large, somewhere between seventy and ninety people. The location of the site on an outer exposed coast is also unusual. It faces Labrador and the Strait of Belle Isle, instead of being situated in much more sheltered coves east of Cape Bauld, so

*Viking and visitors by the replica houses of L'Anse aux Meadows.*
Photo: Department of Tourism Culture and Recreation

evidently it was the Strait that was of the greatest concern among the inhabitants.

While there is no other Norse site like that of the L'Anse aux Meadows site, there is one known from literature that is its perfect match: Straumfjord of the Saga of Erik the Red. Like Straumfjord L'Anse aux Meadows was a base for further exploration. The archeological evidence showed that its people had ventured further south to areas where grapes grow wild, in other words, to Hóp. Wild grapes have never grown in Newfoundland. The closest place where they occur is in the Chaleur Bay and Miramichi region of New brunswick. This area also has all the other features described for Hóp.

There is little doubt that L'Anse aux Meadows is the Straumfjord site and the Leifsbúðir of the Saga of the Greenlanders. With Hóp on the southern shore of the Gulf of St. Lawrence, the orientation of L'Anse aux Meadows to the Strait of Belle Isle makes sense. The strait leads into the gulf , which forms an inland sea, which can be circumnavigated beginning and ending at L'Anse aux Meadows. Vinland comprised all the coastal areas around this sea. L'Anse aux Meadows was the main base for exploring and exploiting this rich land.

The large size of the L'Anse aux Meadows settlement and the effort that went into its establishment shows that it must be a site recorded in the sagas. To erect the buildings over 1000 cubic metres of sod had to be cut and 86 trees to be felled for the posts for the big halls, plus all the other wood utilized in

the construction. Anywhere between six weeks and two months would have been needed for the project. This is the better part of one summer. It also took a great part of the entire Greenland population to operate the post. In Leif's and Karlsefni's time, all of Greenland had only about 500 people. Greenland simply did not have the man power to spare for two such places. This is indeed Straumfjord.

## Norstead

Norstead: A Viking Port of Trade was created to take history out of the exhibit case and place it in the hands of visitors. Join costumed interpreters in the dim light of the Viking-style Chieftain's Hall and listen to mysterious Viking tales. Watch the blacksmith forging iron. Step aboard the full-scale replica Viking ship *Snorri*. Learn how the Vikings mastered the North Atlantic. Use a simple notched stick to measure distance by the stars. Shape clay into pottery the way the Vikings did. Spin sheep fleece into yarn using ancient drop spindle technology, dye the yarn bright purple, pink, or rusty yellow using local plants and berries....weave it into cloth at the loom. It's in your hands to explore!

Located about two km from L'Anse aux Meadows National Historic Site, the only authenticated Viking site in North America, Norstead replicates a Viking port of trade as it may have looked during the Viking era (790-1066 AD). The four-hectare site has a boat shed with its very own Viking ships, including the 54 foot replica Viking knarr

*Norstead Village.*                    *Photos: Rögnvaldur Guðmundsson and Rolf Hicker (left corner)*

which sailed from Greenland to L'Anse aux Meadows in 1998 with a crew of only nine men. There is also a chieftain's hall, church, and a workshop, with costumed interpreters who bring the site to life. All buildings, which consist of wood paneled walls and earthen floors, have been created to convey the look and feel of the Viking Era.

Norstead, which won the provincial Attractions Canada award for "Best New Attraction", was the centerpiece of a series of events held in 2000 to mark the 1,000th anniversary of the Vikings' arrival in the New World. Those events generated widespread media coverage and helped the site attract 28,000 visitors in its first season of operation. The aim of the site is to ensure that visitors have the opportunity to gain a broader understanding of Norse life, while having fun through an enriched travel experience. Norstead is open daily from June to September.

## Further information

*www.pc.gc.ca/lhn-nhs/nl/meadows*
*www.norstead.com*
*www.vikingtrail.org*

# Contributors

| Chapters | Authors | Translators |
|---|---|---|
| The Sagalands story | *Rögnvaldur Guðmundsson* | *Anna Benassi* |
| Welcome to the Sagalands route! | *Geir Sør-Reime* | |
| Storytelling in the Nordic world | *Tom Muir* | |
| The Vikings Age, poems and the Icelandic sagas | *Gísli Sigurðsson* | *Bernard Scudder* |
| The Árni Magnússon Institute's Exhibition | *Gísli Sigurðsson* | *Bernard Scudder* |
| The Viking ship Icelander | *Sigrún Ásta Jónsdóttir* | *Anna Benassi* |
| Snorri Sturluson and Egil's Saga | *Hjörleifur Stefánsson and Sigríður M. Guðmundsdóttir* | |
| Eiríksstadir | *Árni Björnsson and Rögnvaldur Guðmundsson* | *Bernard Scudder* |
| The Saga of Gísli Súrsson | *Þórir Örn Guðmundsson and Dorothee Lubecki* | *Sonja Elín Thompson and Micaela Kristin-Kali* |
| The Saga of Grettir the strong | *Pétur Jónsson* | *Anna Benassi* |
| Njál's Saga | *Sigrún R. Ragnarsdóttir* | *Anna Benassi* |
| Thjórsárdalur Valley | *Ásborg Arnþórsdóttir* | *Anna Benassi* |
| The Viking Trail of South Greenland | *Rie Oldenburg and Finn Lynge* | *Kirsten Jexlev* |
| The Faroe Islands and the Færeyinga Saga | *Regin Debess and Símun V. Arge* | |
| Trondenes Historical Centre | *Ole J. Furset* | |
| Lofotr, the Vikingmuseum at Borg | *Wenche Brun* | |
| Avaldsnes, Norway's oldest throne | *Karl Johan Gundersen and Marit S. Vea* | |
| Gene Fornby | *Maria Blomster* | |
| The Shetland Islands | *David Cooper* | |
| The Orkney Islands and the Orkneyinga Saga | *Tom Muir* | |
| Isle of Man | *Andrew Foxon* | |
| L'Anse aux Meadows | *Birgitta Wallace* | |